Leckie × Leckie

Help your child with Maths

Makes Maths make sense!

Jeanette Mumford

01/240611

ISBN 978-1-84372-894-8

Published by
Leckie & Leckie Ltd
An imprint of HarperCollins*Publishers*
Westerhill Road, Bishopbriggs, Glasgow, G64 2QT
T: 0844 576 8126 F: 0844 576 8131
leckieandleckie@harpercollins.co.uk www.leckieandleckie.co.uk

Special thanks to
Roda Morrison (copy-edit), Helen Bleck (proofread), Jan Fisher (proofread), Caleb O'Loan (technical proofread), Edward Mullan (technical proofread), Planman Technologies (layout and illustration)

A CIP Catalogue record for this book is available from the British Library.

MIX
Paper from responsible sources
FSC® C007454

FSC is a non-profit international organisation established to promote the responsible management of the world's forests. Products carrying the FSC label are independently certified to assure consumers that they come from forests that are managed to meet the social, economic and ecological needs of present and future generations.

Find out more about HarperCollins and the environment at
www.harpercollins.co.uk/green

Contents

How to get the most from Help Your Child with Maths....

Top Tip for Parents

Check up Tasks are provided to help you assess how well your child has understood each topic.

Help Your Child with Maths is written for you and your child to work through together at home to grow your child's maths ability. It's the perfect solution for every parent wanting to make certain that his or her child is up to speed with maths. With clear guidance to help children of all abilities practise and learn, **Help Your Child with Maths** has masses of creative activities to make learning maths fun, even for the most restless child!

What this book contains...

Help Your Child with Maths is aligned to Scotland's **Curriculum for Excellence** to make certain that your child is learning exactly the right maths at the right time. It covers all maths topics included in **Level 2** of the curriculum, routinely studied by children between the ages of 9 and 12, though also sometimes by younger and older learners. Children studying at KS2 will also find this a useful resource. **Help Your Child with Maths** provides invaluable assistance for children during the transition from primary to secondary school – when children can struggle to keep up with maths.

Make learning fun!

Every topic of **Help Your Child with Maths** is packed full of fun activities. Designed to help your child's understanding of maths, the activities are highly creative, providing many varied opportunities to practise maths.

Whether you want to help with homework or build on what your child is learning in class, **Help Your Child with Maths** covers all the core subjects. This simple step by step approach makes certain that learning isn't a chore for your child and that maths makes sense!

The book's activities encourage your child to practise maths, often with a friend or an adult. Working in pairs on activities is a great approach not only to learning through talking about maths but also to retaining interest. The activities are both challenging and creative, and have very clear links to real-life situations showing how much maths matters all around us in our environment.

op Tips for Parents

- Find a quiet, comfortable place to work, away from other distractions.
- Ask your child what Maths they are doing at school and choose an appropriate topic.
- Tackle one topic at a time.
- Help with reading where necessary, and ensure your child understands what to do.
- Help and encourage your child to check their own answers as they complete each activity.
- Discuss with your child what they have learned.
- Let your child return to their favourite page once it has been completed, to play the games and talk about the activities with you or a partner.
- Reward your child with plenty of praise and encouragement.
- Additional resources can be found on the Leckie & Leckie website at www.leckieandleckie.co.uk and can be downloaded free of charge.

our child will also find it helpful if they have to hand:

- Calculator
- Ruler
- Supply of pencils
- 1 cm squared paper
- 0–9 digit cards (these can be downloaded from the "Help Your Child with Maths" page on the Leckie & Leckie website)

Answers

nd last but not least, answers to all questions are found on pages 88–101.

> **Note:** Throughout the book you will come across two types of equals sign.
> = means equals
> ≈ means approximately equals

Place value in numbers

Top Tip for Parents

Some children are confused by the signs $<$ and $>$ for less than and greater than. Say to your child: The open part of the sign always faces the larger number.

Example: *7p is more or greater than 4p so 7 tenths is greater than 4 tenths.*

$4·7 > 4·1$
4·7 is greater than 4·1
$4·1 < 4·7$
4·1 is less than 4·7

In everyday life there are many situations where we have to read, write and order large numbers and decimal numbers.

When writing large numbers we usually insert commas, e.g. 1,234,567. However, in printed text, we usually find that each comma is replaced by a space, e.g. 1 234 567. Calculators will show this number as 1234567.

1 000 000	one million
100 000	one hundred thousand
10 000	ten thousand
1 000	one thousand
100	one hundred
10	ten
1	one
0·1	one tenth
0·01	one hundredth
0·001	one thousandth

The decimal point separates the whole numbers from the decimal numbers.

In the number 1 234 567·09:

- the 3 is in the ten thousands place. The 3 is worth 30 000;
- the 9 is in the hundredths place. The 9 represents 9 hundredths or 0·09;
- the 0 is a place holder and shows that there are no tenths in the number.

Exercises

1 Ask your child to read each whole and each decimal number aloud. Then ask, *What does the red digit represent in each number?*

a 1 432 198 b 9 609 123 c 6 987 014

d 2 506 000 e 1 375·84 f 492·06

2 Write the sign $<$ (is less than) or $>$ (is greater than) to make each statement correct.

Example
$4·7 < 4·9$
$6·9 > 6·79$

a 5·2 □ 5·4 b 0·39 □ 0·37 c 2·14 □ 2·78

d 3·42 □ 3·5 e 7·17 □ 7·7 f 6·0 □ 5·19

3 The six best distances recorded in the Welly Boot Throwing Competition were:

34·27 m 33·85 m 35·05 m 34·69 m 31·41 m 32·96 m

Which distance won:

a first prize? 35·05 b second prize?  c third prize? 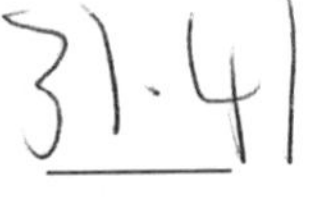

Go and do!

1 **Decimals in order An activity for two players**

Each person uses the digits 4, 5 and 8 to make six numbers with one, two or three decimal places then orders their numbers, starting with the smallest.

My numbers	In order (smallest → largest)	Partner's numbers	In order (smallest → largest)
0·		0·	
0·		0·	
0·		0·	
0·		0·	
0·		0·	
0·		0·	

Take it in turns to choose a number with two or three decimal places from your ordered column of numbers and ask your partner to find the nearest number in his or her ordered column of numbers which is smaller than (or larger than) your number.

2 **All the fours Challenge task!**

Each umbrella shows a decimal number to 3 decimal places.

- Find how many decimal numbers to 3 decimal places lie between 2·4 and 2·5.
- How many of these decimal numbers
  - have one 4? Which are they?
  - have two 4s? Which are they?
  - have three 4s? Which are they?

Check up tasks

Help! Keep Going! Good to go!

Ask your child: *Which is the smaller number – 5·56 or 5·52? How did you work it out?*

Ask your child: *Can you tell me a decimal number that lies between 3·71 and 3·79? Is your number closer to 3·71 or to 3·79? How do you know?*

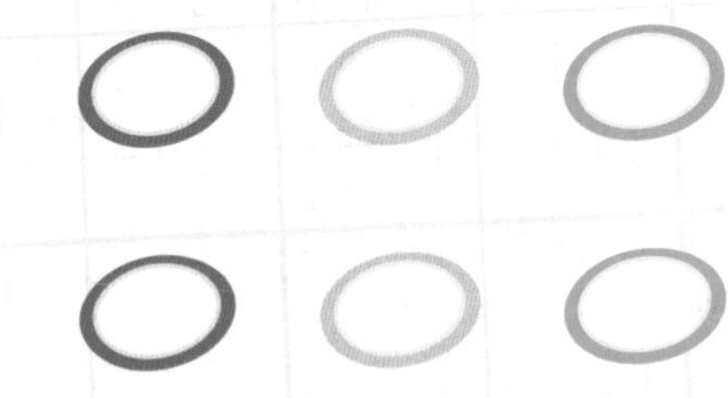

Rounding and estimating

We often round numbers when we want to find an approximate answer. Numbers rounded to the nearest 10,100 or 1000 are easier to work with, to remember, to estimate an answer and to check our working out.

Cost of car = £12 758 → £12 760 to the nearest 10
£12 800 to the nearest 100
£13 000 to the nearest 1000

Rules for rounding

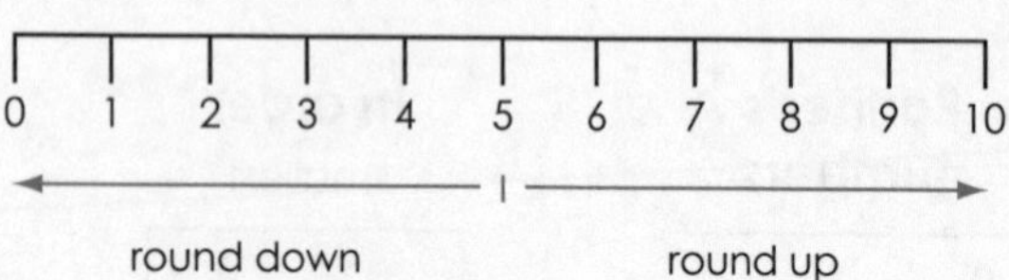

- The digits ending in a 1, 2, 3 or 4 always round down.
- The digits ending in a 5, 6, 7, 8 or 9 always round up.
- 5·174 correct to two decimal places is 5·17.
- 5·174 correct to one decimal place is 5·2.
- 5·174 correct to the nearest whole number is 5.

Estimation and approximation

An estimate is a sensible guess. Suppose you need to work out 58 + 79. You can estimate that your answer will be less than 60 + 80 or less than 140.

An approximation is an answer which is 'near enough'. For example, approximately how much do six bags of sweets at 95p each cost? Since 95p is nearly £1 then 6 × 95p is nearly 6 × £1 or £6.

Top Tip for Parents

If your child is having difficulty when rounding decimals with two places to the nearest whole number, e.g. 4·57 you can help by sketching a number line

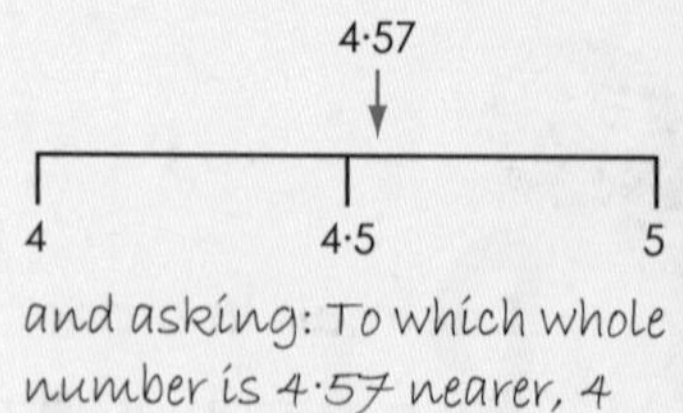

and asking: To which whole number is 4·57 nearer, 4 or 5?

Exercises

1 Round each of these numbers:

	Number	To the nearest 10	To the nearest 100	To the nearest 1000
a	6985			
b	9658			
c	56 098			
d	68 905			
e	650 981			
f	605 189			
g	1 986 506			
h	1 869 519			

Round each price to the nearest pound.

a £6·45 £☐ b £7·79 £☐ c £3·18 £☐ d £13·43 £☐

Estimate the perimeter of each regular polygon to the nearest centimetre by first rounding the length of a side.

Hint: A regular polygon has all sides equal.

a

Perimeter ≈ _______ cm

b

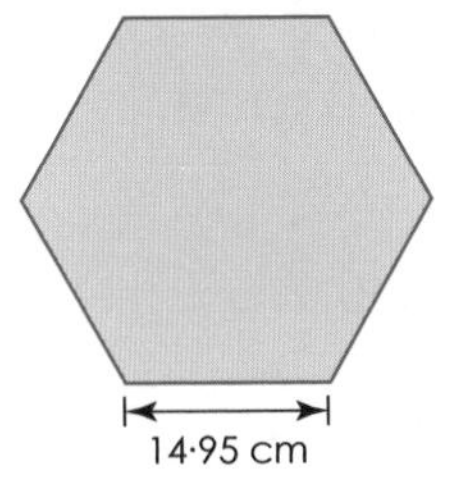

Perimeter ≈ _______ cm

c

12·25 cm

Perimeter ≈ _______ cm

Go and do!

Round to a whole number **A game for two players**

You need

- One set of 0–9 digit cards
- One decimal point card each
- Score card

- Shuffle the digit cards and place them face down in a pile.
- On your turn take the top three cards and, using the decimal point card, make a number with two decimal places, e.g. 4·59.
- Round your decimal to the nearest whole number, i.e. 5. That is your score for the round.
- Add up your score after 10 rounds. The winner is the player with the larger total.

What if … you choose four digit cards to make a number with three decimal places?

Go and find!

Example

USA 1·5435
This means that £1 = $1·54 or 1 dollar and 54 cents.
£100 will buy $154.

- Switch on your TV to BBC 1 or BBC 2. Go to Teletext page 240, Foreign Exchange. Select Tourist Rates. This will give you the currency selling rates for today.
- Choose 10 different countries from the list on the Teletext page(s). For each country, find what £1 is worth to two decimal places and what £100 will buy in that country's currency.

Check up tasks

Ask your child: *What is 3·45 rounded to one decimal place? To the nearest whole number?*

Say to your child: *In my purse I have £8 in coins, rounded to the nearest pound. What is the largest/smallest amount of money I could have in my purse?*

In your head (1)

Skill in adding or subtracting mentally whole numbers or decimals requires that we understand place value and rounding and have a quick recall of addition facts.

If we know the sum of two whole numbers then we can derive the decimal facts, e.g.

70 + 56 = 126
7·0 + 5·6 = 12·6
0·7 + 0·56 = 1·26

Top Tip for Parents

Encourage your child to become proficient in these skills when calculating mentally.

1. We can split 86 + 38 into these parts: 86 + 30 + 8. 86 plus 30 is 116. Add 8 makes 124.
2. We can change £5·95 + £8·99 to £6 and £9 by adding 5p and 1p to the amounts respectively. £6 plus £9 is £15 less 6p, the amount added on, which is £14·94.

Exercises

1 Work out these answers in your head.

a Find the sum of the numbers in the triangles coloured:

red ______ white ______ blue ______

b Find the difference between the numbers in the triangles coloured:

yellow ______ green ______ purple ______

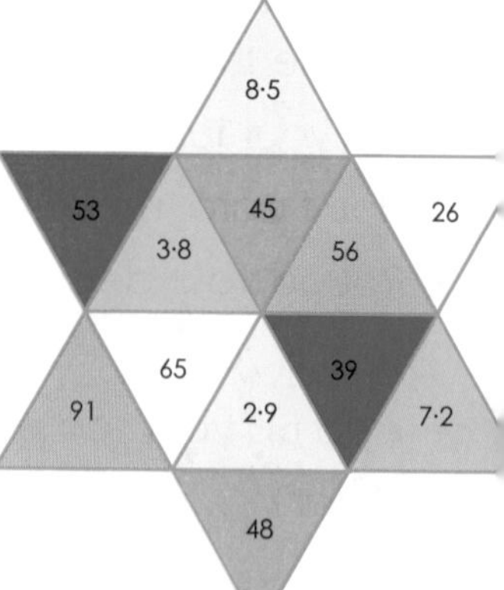

c Find the totals and differences for these numbers on the star.

Complete the table.

Numbers	Total	Difference
Two highest whole numbers		
Two lowest whole numbers		
Two highest decimal numbers		
Two lowest decimal numbers		
Highest and lowest odd and whole numbers		
Highest and lowest even and whole numbers		

2 In this stone wall each stone is related to its supporting stones by the same rule.
Complete these stone walls.

Example

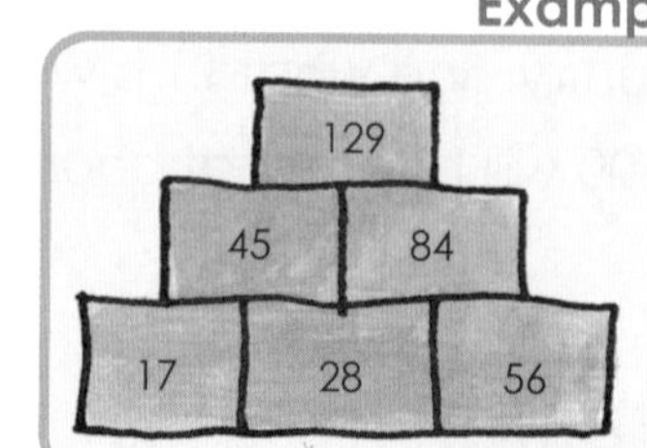

→ 129 − 45 = 84

Check by adding:

45 + 84 = 129

a

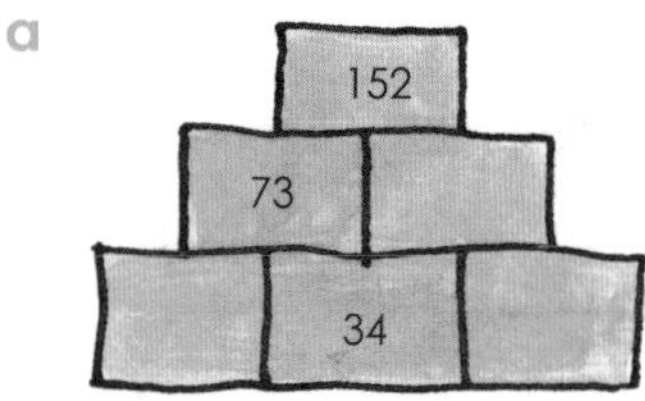

b

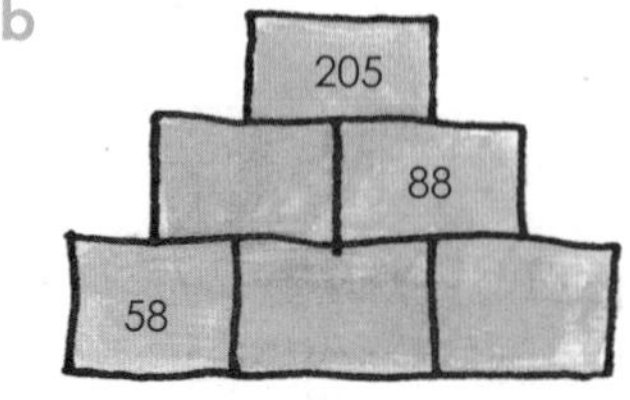

c

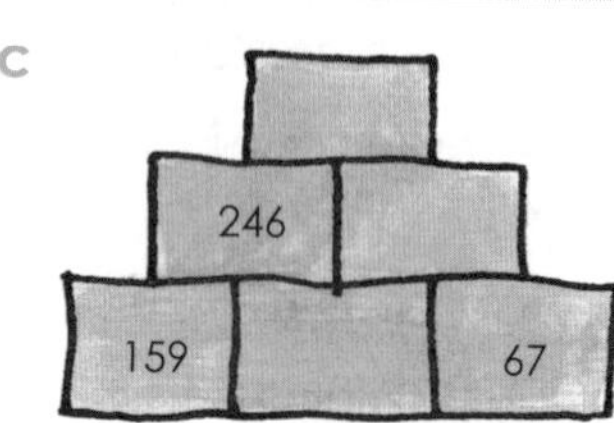

Go and do!

1 • Use four digits 5, 6, 7 and 8 and place them in the grid.
• Multiply the adjacent numbers.
• Total the products.
30 + 40 + 56 + 42 = 168

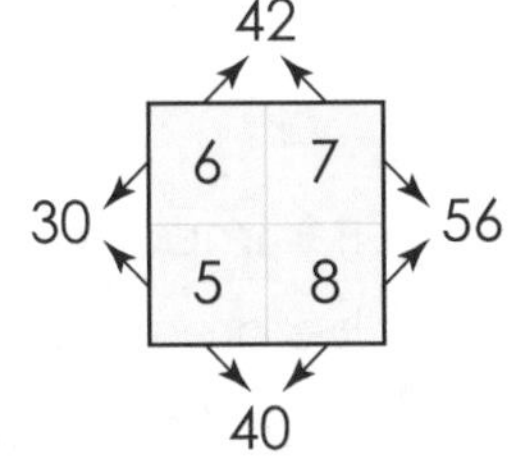

Change the position of the digits 5, 6, 7 and 8 in the grid.
What is the largest and smallest total you can make?

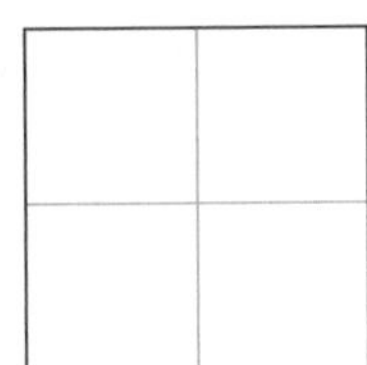
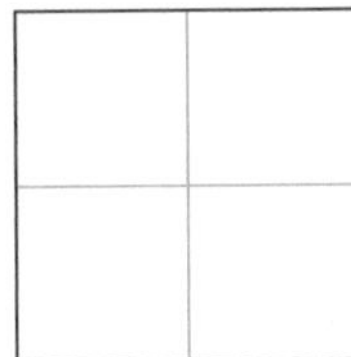
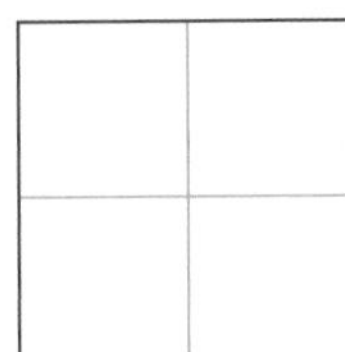

The largest total ______ The smallest total ______

2 Use any four of these digits once.
Arrange them to make two decimal numbers that total 10.
□·□ + □·□ = 10
Investigate different ways to complete the statement using any four different digits.

3 Continue this pattern as far as you can go.

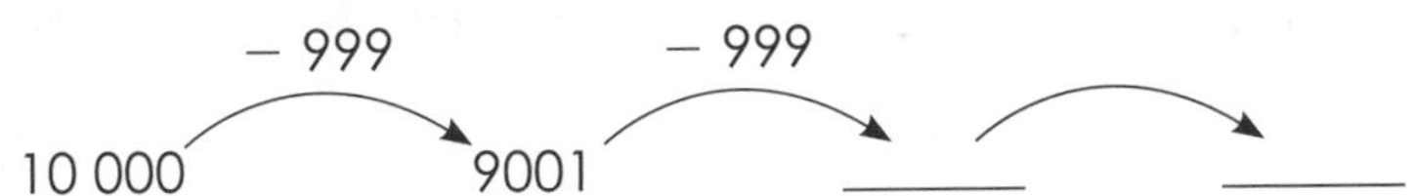

Check up tasks

Ask your child: *You have £17·60. How much do you need to make £50? How did you work it out? What if you need to make £100?*

Ask your child: *What is a quick way to subtract 999? Can you describe the pattern you found in question 3 of 'Go and do!'?*

Add and subtract

Top Tip for Parents

Check that your child has written an approximate answer before beginning a calculation as this will give your child a 'feel' of where the answer should lie.

It is important that we work out an approximate answer before we begin a calculation. This 'good guess' can then be used to check the answer and is particularly helpful when we work with decimals.

Written method for vertical addition

6 add 9 is 15. That is 1 ten and 5 units.
2 tens add 3 tens add 1 ten is 6 tens.
8 hundred add 4 hundred is 12 hundred.
That is 1 thousand and 2 hundred.
4 thousand add 6 thousand add 1 thousand is 11 thousand.

4826 + 6439
Approximate: 11 000

$$\begin{array}{r} 4826 \\ +\ 6439 \\ \hline 11265 \\ \hline {\scriptstyle 11} \end{array}$$

Written methods for vertical subtraction

8357 − 2614
Approximate: 5 000

Expanded method

$$\begin{array}{rcccccc} & {\scriptstyle 7000} & & {\scriptstyle 1300} & & & \\ & \cancel{8000} & + & \cancel{300} & + & 50 & + 7 \\ - & 2000 & + & 600 & + & 10 & + 4 \\ \hline & 5000 & + & 700 & + & 40 & + 3 \end{array}$$

Standard column method

$$\begin{array}{r} {\scriptstyle 7\ 13} \\ \cancel{8}\cancel{3}57 \\ -\ 2614 \\ \hline 5743 \end{array}$$

Exercises

1 First find the approximate answer. Then find the exact total or difference setting out each calculation in columns. Remember to align the decimal points.

a 3641 + 5283 = 8924	b 9263 + 785 = 10048	c 7529 + 86 + 604 = 8219
d 12·49 + 9·27 28·6	e 36·54 + 9·8	f 147·0 + 10·49 + 0·67
g 8319 − 4256 = 4063	h 7940 − 5882 = 2062	i 7204 − 727 = 6517
j 84·6 − 64·8 = 19·8	k 23·05 − 7·42 = 18·43	l 33·5 − 8·75

Go and do!

1 All the nines **A game for two players**

<table><tr><td>You need
• Two sets of 0–9 digit cards</td></tr></table>

- Shuffle the cards. Deal four cards to each player.
- Make a 4-digit number with your cards.
- Add 3876 to your number.
- You score 1 point for each 9 in your answer.
- The first player to reach 9 points is the winner.

```
  5143
+ 3876
  9019
  ↑  ↑   Score: 2 points
```

2 Give me a 10

Find as many different ways as you can of completing the addition statement.

You cannot use a digit more than once in each calculation. □·□ + □·□ = 10

Score: 10 or more – excellent

8–10 – very good

Note: Since 4·7 + 5·3 = 10 is the same as 5·3 + 4·7 = 10 this counts as one way.

3 Same digits, different totals

<table><tr><td>You need
• Digit cards 1, 2, 3, 4, 5 and 6</td></tr></table>

Make two 3-digit numbers with your digits so that their sum equals these totals.

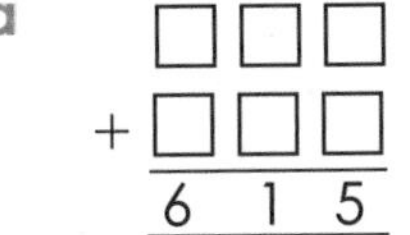

```
a   □□□        b   □□□        c   □□□        d   □□□
  + □□□          + □□□          + □□□          + □□□
    6 1 5          8 9 4          3 9 9          3 8 1
```

4 Missing digits

Work out the missing digits in these subtractions.

```
a   6 5 4 3 2     b   8 7 6 5 4     c   7 6 5 4 3     d   9 8 7 6 5
  − 4 □ □ 7 □       − □ 1 □ □ 6       − 4 □ 9 □ □       − □ 1 □ 7 □
    2 3 4 5 6         4 5 6 7 8         3 4 5 6 7         5 6 7 8 9
```

5 Pattern puzzles

a Find the answer to each subtraction.

b Now find the difference between consecutive answers.

c What patterns do you notice?

d What if the pattern began 111·1 − 1·111, 222·2 − 2·222?

11·1 − 1·11 = ____

22·2 − 2·22 = ____

33·3 − 3·33 = ____

44·4 − 4·44 = ____

Check up tasks

Ask your child: *How might you find the approximate answer to 4518 + 1937? To 48·76 − 16·35?*

Ask your child: *How did you go about finding the missing digits in 'Go and do!' question 3?*

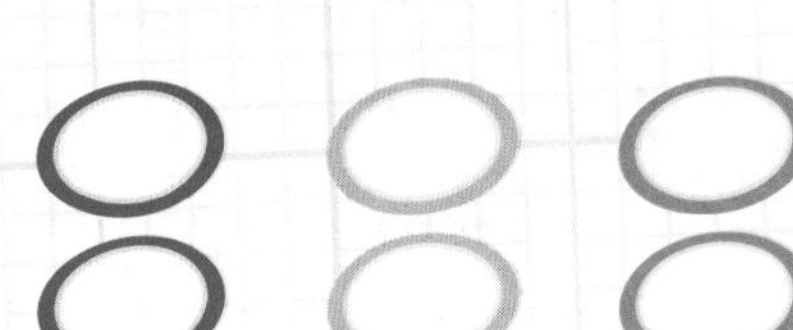

Ask your child: *What patterns did you notice in question 4?*

In your head (2)

If we know our times tables up to 10 x 10 and understand place value then we can use multiplication and decimal facts to work out mentally other facts involving decimals and multiples of 10 or 100.

$6 \times 8 = 48$	$0{\cdot}6 \times 8 = 4{\cdot}8$	$6 \times 80 = 480$
$8 \times 6 = 48$	$0{\cdot}8 \times 6 = 4{\cdot}8$	$8 \times 60 = 480$
$48 \div 6 = 8$	$4{\cdot}8 \div 6 = 0{\cdot}8$	$480 \div 6 = 80$
$48 \div 8 = 6$	$4{\cdot}8 \div 8 = 0{\cdot}6$	$480 \div 80 = 6$

We can use the items we buy at the supermarket to give our child practice in multiplying and dividing mentally; e.g. a box of 6 eggs costs £1·50. How much for 1 egg? A tin of beans costs 41p. How much will 10 tins cost? 5 tins?

Top Tip for Parents

When you ask a child what happens to a number when you multiply it by 10 the usual response is, 'add a zero', e.g. 6 × 10 = 60. As a result some children mistakenly think that dividing by 10 is simply removing a zero. This can cause confusion when they divide numbers that result in decimal answers, e.g. 827 ÷ 10 = 82·7.

Exercises

1 Write three facts you can derive from each of these statements.

a $30 \times 7 = 210$

____

____

____

b $720 \div 90 = 8$

____

____

____

c $0{\cdot}9 \times 5 = 4{\cdot}5$

____

____

____

Example

$40 \times 30 = 1200$
$1200 \div 4 = 300$
$1{\cdot}2 \div 3 = 0{\cdot}4$
$3 \times 400 = 1200$

2 Rule 1: *To multiply by 50, first multiply by 100 then divide by 2.*
Rule 2: *To multiply by 25, first multiply by 100 then divide by 4.*
Use the rules to buy the amounts shown for each item.

Buy	× £1·60
10	
100	
50	
25	

Buy	× £0·46
10	
100	
50	
60	

Buy	× £7
100	
500	
250	
400	

£1·60

46p

£7

3 A school bought these items for the PE store. Working in your head, complete the bill from the sports shop:

5 netballs @ ________	each	£115·00
10 skittles @ ________	each	£79·90
6 softballs @ ________	each	£96·00
8 footballs @ ________	each	£280·00

Go and do!

You need

- Two sets of 2–9 digit cards

1 **Running totals** **A game for two players**

- Copy this score sheet. Write each player's name at the top.
- Shuffle the digit cards. Deal two cards to each player.
- On your turn, find the product of the two numbers, e.g. cards 5 and 9 → $5 \times 9 = 45$. Record your score.
- On your next turn, add your second score to the first and record the total, e.g. $4 \times 6 = 24$. $24 + 45 = 69$.
- The first player to reach 250 is the winner.

2 **By 10, by 100, by 1000**

You need

- Digit cards 2, 4, 7 and 9

- Use your digit cards to make, in turn, two 2-digit, two 3-digit and two 4-digit numbers.
- Multiply each of your numbers by 10, by 100 and by 1000. Divide each of your numbers by 10 and by 100.
- Record your answers in the table.

Number	× 10	× 100	× 1000	÷ 10	÷ 100
47	470	4700	47 000	4·7	0·47

3 **On the cards**

You need

- Digit cards 3, 5 and 8

- Using the digit cards 3, 5 and 8, make six different multiplications like this. □·□ × □
- What is the largest product you can make? The smallest?
- What if the multiplication was like this? □·□ × □

Check up tasks

Help! Keep Going! Good to go!

Select and price some items and multipacks from your kitchen cupboard, e.g. jar of jam, 10 pack of KitKat biscuits. Then ask your child questions such as: *What is the cost of three jars of jam? A single biscuit?*

Using brackets

Top Tip for Parents

Check that your child knows the order of operations, i.e. brackets first, then multiplication and division followed by addition and subtraction.

If your child makes errors in doubling an answer twice you could suggest that making some jottings in table form would be useful.

$23{\cdot}4 \times 1 = 23{\cdot}4$
$23{\cdot}4 \times 2 = 46{\cdot}8$
$23{\cdot}4 \times 3 = 70{\cdot}2$
$23{\cdot}4 \times 4 = 93{\cdot}6$

There are two ways of doing these calculations:

$7 + 3 \times 8$ and $7 \times 6 - 2$.

$7 + 3 \times 8 = 10 \times 8 = 80$ or $= 7 + 24 = 31$

$7 \times 6 - 2 = 42 - 2 = 40$ or $= 7 \times 4 = 28$

But which answer is correct? There is an established order of operations, namely:

Always multiply or divide first before you add or subtract unless there are brackets. If there are brackets, do what is inside the brackets first.

To avoid any confusion, we put brackets around what is to be multiplied or divided.

$7 + (3 \times 8) = 7 + 24 = 31$

$(7 \times 6) - 2 = 42 - 2 = 40$

Some numbers can be made easier to calculate using doubling (multiply by 2) or halving (divide by 2). We double or halve the numbers in order of significance.

Double the hundreds first, then the tens, then the units and add them together.

Double $238 = (200 \times 2) + (30 \times 2) + (8 \times 2) = 400 + 60 + 16 = 476$

Halve $87 = (80 \div 2) + (7 \div 2) = 40 + 3{\cdot}5 = 43{\cdot}5$

Exercises

1 Insert two pairs of brackets each time and find the answer to the calculation.

a $2 + 5 \times 4 - 3 \times 6$ ______________________

b $2 + 5 \times 4 - 3 \times 6$ ______________________

c $2 + 5 \times 4 - 3 \times 6$ ______________________

2 Use the digits 4, 6 and 8 to complete each calculation.

a $(\square \times \square) - \square = 16$

b $(\square \times \square) \div \square = 3$

c $\square + (\square \times \square) = 32$

d $\square - (\square \div \square) = 4$

Complete the number statements using +, −, × or ÷ in each box.

a (12 □ 3) + (4 □ 5) = 24 b (12 □ 3) − (4 □ 5) = 16

c (5 × 4) □ (3 + 2) □ 1 = 5 d (5 □ 43) □ 21 = 27

Complete these doubling patterns.

a		b		c	
1 × 8 =	8	1 × 15 =	15	1 × 23 =	23
2 × 8 =	16	2 × 15 =	30	2 × 23 =	
4 × 8 =	32	4 × 15 =	60	4 × 23 =	
8 × 8 =	56	8 × 15 =	120	8 × 23 =	
16 × 8 =		16 × 15 =		16 × 23 =	

We can use doubling to multiply large numbers by 4. Work out the answers to these calculations.

Example

432 × 4
double 432 → 864
double 864 → 1728

a 162 × 4
double → ______
double → ______

b 807 × 4
double → ______
double → ______

c 23·4 × 4
double → ______
double → ______

Work out the answers by halving one number and doubling the other.

a 8 × 7·5
4 × 15 = 60

b 12 × 6·5
□ × □ = □

c 18 × 3·5
□ × □ = □

d 24 × 2·5
□ × □ = □

e 16 × 4·5
□ × □ = □

f 30 × 5·5
□ × □ = □

Go and do!

1 **Even more brackets**

- Use the even digit numbers 2, 4, 6 and 8. (□ + □) × (□ + □) =
- Arrange the four digits in the calculation and solve it.
- Rearrange your four digits. How many different calculations can you make?

Check up tasks

Ask your child: *How would you go about finding the answer to the calculation, 4 + 6 × 7 − 3? How do you know that you have the correct answer?*

Multiplication methods

Top Tip for Parents

Some children can struggle with the standard short multiplication method. The best way for you to approach this is to let your child continue with the expanded short multiplication method and, once your child feels sufficiently secure, move on to the more efficient and standard method.

Short multiplication

The term short multiplication is applied to the multiplication of 2, 3 or more digits by a single digit, e.g. 473×6. Your child should have a secure understanding of the informal methods (1–3) before progressing to the standard method (4).

The following vocabulary is common to the worked examples 1 to 3.

- *Split 473 times 6 into three calculations, 400 times 6, 70 times 6 and 3 times 6.*
- *400 times 6 equals 2400; 70 times 7 equals 420; 3 times 6 is 18.*
- *Add the units (8), the tens (30), the hundreds (800) and the thousands (2000). The answer is 2838.*

1 Using a grid

×	6
400	2400
70	420
3	18
	2838

2 Using partitioning

$473 \times 6 = (400 \times 6) + (70 \times 6) + (3 \times 6)$
$= 2400 + 420 + 18$
$= 2838$

3 Expanded short multiplication

$$\begin{array}{rl} 473 & \\ \times\ 6 & \\ \hline 2400 & (400 \times 6) \\ 420 & (70 \times 6) \\ 18 & (3 \times 6) \\ \hline 2838 & \\ \hline \end{array}$$

4 Standard short multiplication

$473 \times 6 \approx 500 \times 6 \approx 3000$

$$\begin{array}{r} 473 \\ \times\ 6 \\ \hline 2838 \\ \hline {\scriptstyle 4\ 1} \end{array}$$

- 3 times 6 is 18. That is 1 ten and 8 units.
- 7 tens times 6 is 42 tens. Add 1 ten is 43 tens. That is 4 hundreds and 3 tens
- 4 hundred times 6 is 24 hundred. Add 4 hundred is 28 hundred. That is 2 thousand 8 hundred.

Exercises

1 Approximate your answer first. Then use a multiplication method to work out the answer to each calculation.

a 83×6 b 47×5 c 254×8

d 169×9 e 768×4 f 429×7

2 a Work out the answers to these calculations.

$22 \times 9 =$ ______ $44 \times 9 =$ ______ $66 \times 9 =$ ______

b Look for a pattern in your answers to 2a and predict the answers for:

$55 \times 9 =$ ______ $77 \times 9 =$ ______ $99 \times 9 =$ ______

Using partitioning, complete the answers to these calculations.

a $14{\cdot}3 \times 14 = (14{\cdot}3 \times 7) + (14{\cdot}3 \times 7) =$ ______ + ______ = ______

b $14{\cdot}3 \times 21 = (14{\cdot}3 \times 7) + (14{\cdot}3 \times 14) =$ ______ + ______ = ______

c $14{\cdot}3 \times 28 =$ ______________________________

Look for a pattern and predict the answers for:

d $14{\cdot}3 \times 35 =$ ______ e $14{\cdot}3 \times 49 =$ ______ f $14{\cdot}3 \times 63 =$ ______

Go and do!

You need
- Calculator

Rugby Sevens **A game for two players**

- Take turns to choose a number from a boot and a number from a rugby ball.
- Multiply the two numbers together. Check using a calculator.
- If the answer is less than 500 you score a try: 3 points.
  If the answer is more than 500 you score a try and conversion: 5 points.
- Play seven rounds then total your points.
- Scoring: over 25 points: excellent, 20–24 points: very good.

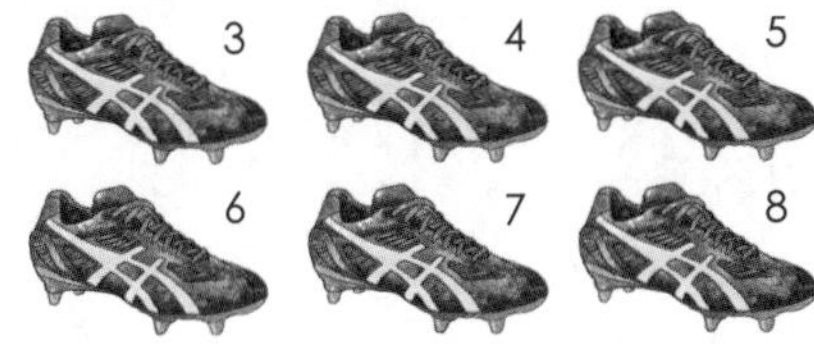

You need
- Calculator

Calculator tricks

- Put any 3-digit number into your calculator.
- Multiply this number by 13.
- Now multiply the answer by 11.
- Finally multiply the answer by 7.

What do you notice about the answer?
Investigate the trick using different 3-digit numbers.
Can you explain why it works?

Check up tasks

Ask your child: *Describe the pattern you found in Exercises question 2. Can you use it to find 88 × 9?*

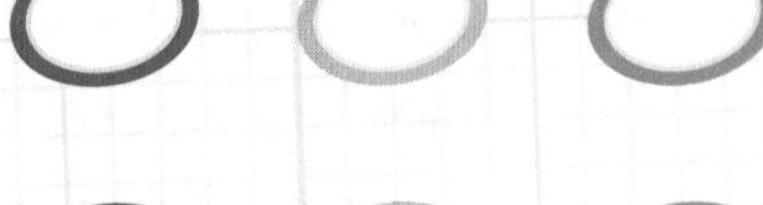

Ask your child: *Look at question 3. How does the pattern help you find 14·3 × 63?*

Division methods

Top Tip for Parents

Having a sound knowledge of 'Times Tables' facts is key to success in division where your child has to identify the multiple of a number which is closest to the divisor, e.g. 56 is the multiple of 8 closest to 59.

Short division

We apply the term short division to the division of 2, 3 or more digits by a single digit, e.g. 257 ÷ 8. Your child should have a secure understanding of the informal methods before progressing to the standard method.

Division by repeated subtraction

257 ÷ 8 ≈ 240 ÷ 8 ≈ 30

```
8)257
 − 80   (8 × 10)
  177
 − 80   (8 × 10)
   97
 − 80   (8 × 10)
   17
  −16   (8 × 2)
    1         32
```

Answer 32 R 1

Expanded short division

257 ÷ 8 ≈ 240 ÷ 8 ≈ 30

```
8 )257
 − 240   (8 × 30)
    17
  − 16   (8 × 2)
     1         32
```

Answer 32 R 1

'R' means 'remainder'

Standard short division

- *Since 2 is not a multiple of 8 we look at the hundreds and tens together.*
- *24 is the multiple of 8 closest to 25.*
- *25 tens divided by 8 is 3 tens and 1 ten left over.*
- *1 ten added to 7 units is 17. 17 divided by 8 is 2 remainder 1. The answer is 32 R 1.*

```
    32 R 1          3 2 R 1
8 )257           8)25¹7
   24
   17
   16
    1
```

Exercises

1 Approximate your answer and find how many pupils went on each school trip.

	Destination	Cost of trip	Cost per pupil
a	Falkirk Wheel	£156	£6
b	Edinburgh Castle	£294	£7
c	Glasgow Science Centre	£440	£8
d	Deep Sea World	£252	£9
e	New Lanark	£370	£5
f	Loch Ness Centre	£432	£9
g	Blair Drummond Safari Park	£528	£8
h	Butterfly and Insect World	£312	£6

Example

Stirling Castle £258
Cost per pupil £6
258 ÷ 6 ≈ 240 ÷ 6 ≈ 40

```
    43             4 3
6 )258   or   6 )25¹8
  −24
   18
  −18
    0
```

Loch Leckie Seafoods sells its king prawns in trays of 10.
Calculate how many trays are filled.
Write the remainder as a fraction and a decimal.

Example

$72 \div 10 = 7\frac{2}{10}$
$= 7{\cdot}2$
7 trays filled

a 164 prawns

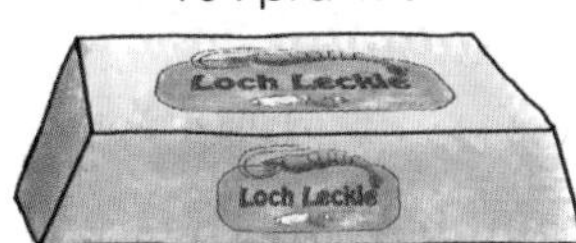

b 286 prawns

c 595 prawns

d 708 prawns

e 574 prawns

f 1209 prawns

Go and do!

Puzzle time

a I am thinking of a two digit number. When I divide it by 6 it has a remainder of 3. When I divide it by 5 it has a remainder of 2. What is my number? ☐

b I am thinking of a two digit number. When I divide it by 8 it has a remainder of 4. When I divide it by 7 it has a remainder of 5. What is my number? ☐

Work out the missing digits.

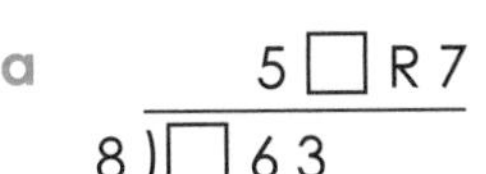

a 8) ☐ 6 3 = 5 ☐ R 7

b ☐) 3 4 9 = 6 ☐ R ☐

c 6) 2 0 8 · ☐ = ☐ 4 · 8

Rearrange each set of four numbers in the form ☐☐☐ ÷ ☐ to make the answer.

a 4, 0, 4, 3 = 76

b 9, 8, 5, 5 = 65

Go and find!

Choose one of the places in question 1 that you would like to visit with your family. Work out the cost for your family day out. Include the following:

- Entrance fees (if any) for adults and children and cost of travel.
- Can you get an 'Away Day Family Ticket' if you travel by public transport?
- If you go by car, calculate the mileage for the round trip at 40p per mile.

Check up tasks

Help! Keep Going! Good to go!

Ask your child: *How did you work out how many pupils went on the trip to the Glasgow Science Centre?*

Ask your child: *If Loch Leckie Seafoods had 1697 king prawns to pack, how many trays would they fill?*

Divisibility

Divisibility tests are used in mathematics to check if one number can be divided exactly by another; for example, when you are finding factors (see pages 26–27) or reducing fractions to their lowest terms by cancelling (see pages 30–31) or simply carrying out a division calculation.

Top Tip for Parents

If your child is finding difficulty in applying the divisibility rule for 8, e.g. 528 ÷ 8, recall that division is the inverse of multiplication so 8 ÷ 2 = 4, 4 ÷ 2 = 2 and 2 ÷ 2 = 1. The task becomes easier if you simplify the recording, e.g.

1 528 ÷ 2 = 264
2 264 ÷ 2 = 132
3 132 ÷ 2 = 66

Tests of divisibility

A number is divisible by:

2 if the last digit is 0, 2, 4, 6 or 8.
3 if the sum of the digits is divisible by 3.
4 if the last two digits are divisible by 4.
5 if the last digit is 5 or 0.
6 if it is divisible by both 2 and 3.
8 if half of it is divisible by 4 or if the last 3 digits are divisible by 8.
9 if the sum of the digits is divisible by 9.
10 if the last digit is 0.

Exercises

1

501	502	503	504	505	506	507	508	509	510
511	512	513	514	515	516	517	518	519	520
521	522	523	524	525	526	527	528	529	530
531	532	533	534	535	536	537	538	539	540
541	542	543	544	545	546	547	548	549	550

You need
- Red and blue pencils

Key
Red – divisible by 3
Blue – divisible by 4

a Colour half of each square in the grid where the number is divisible by 3 or 4.

b Use the tests of divisibility to list the numbers that are divisible:

- by 3 ____________________
- by 4 ____________________

c Now use the tests of divisibility to list the numbers that are divisible:

- by 6 ____________________
- by 8 ____________________
- by 6 and by 8 ____________________

d Using these facts, 2 × 6 = 12 and 3 × 4 = 12, can you find numbers in the grid that are exactly divisible by 12? ____________________

A line of counters is set in a continuous pattern like this:

What is the colour of:

a the 18th counter? ________ b the 39th counter? ________

c the 51st counter? ________ d the 93rd counter? ________

What if the pattern was like this? 

What is the colour of:

e the 18th counter? ________ f the 39th counter? ________

g the 51st counter? ________ h the 93rd counter? ________

There is no general rule to test for the divisibility of 7.

However, there is a test of divisibility by 7 for 3-digit numbers.

- Double the hundreds digit.
- Add this to the 2-digit number made from the tens and unit digits.
- Check if the total divides by 7.
- If yes, then the number is divisible by 7.

Example

378
$2 \times 3 = 6$
$6 + 78 = 84$
$84 \div 7 = 12$
378 is divisible by 7

Use the grid on page 22. List the numbers between 501 and 550 that are divisible by 7.

GO! Go and do!

You need

- 2 sets of 2–9 number cards
- 20 counters in two colours

1 **Divisibility check ups** **A game for two players**

102	192	153	138	300	477
117	49	84	136	423	252
96	54	165	133	174	352
870	72	112	207	288	301

Rules

- Shuffle the number cards. On your turn take the top card and find a number on the grid that is divisible by the number on the card.
- Cover the number with a counter in your colour.
- The winner is the first player to cover 10 numbers.

Check up tasks

Ask your child: *Which numbers will divide exactly into 60? What are the first four multiples of 25? Can you tell me a divisibility rule for 25?*

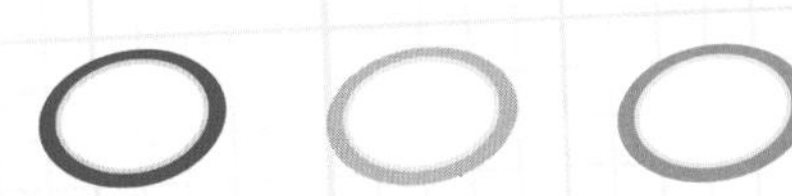

Patterns and puzzles

We hope that as your child explores these patterns and puzzles he or she will find them interesting, challenging and fun and will be encouraged to adopt a more positive and experimental attitude to mathematics.

Top Tip for Parents

In mathematics it is very important that you test a rule more than twice. If you only test it once, or even twice, you could be lucky in that the rule works in these particular cases but it cannot be applied in general.

Exercises

1 **Know your tables**

These multiplication tables are in code.
Each letter represents a different digit.
Work out which multiplication table is represented by

Table O ______ times table

Table Δ ______ times table

Table O
E × A = BF
E × F = CF
E × C = DC
E × H = GC
E × E = AE
E × B = E
E × G = AI
E × D = BD
E × J = CD

Table Δ
Q × P = RX
Q × Q = VU
Q × R = WS
Q × S = XR
Q × T = PT
Q × V = SW
Q × U = Q
Q × W = UV
Q × X = TP

2 **Multiplication patterns**

a Write the next number in: rows 1 to 4 and columns 1 to 4.

b Look for a pattern and complete the numbers in the grid.

c Write how the pattern works for:

row →

column ↓

1	3	5	7	9	11	
2	6	10	14	18		
4	12	20	28	36		
8	24	40	56	72		
16						

Row 1 ______________________ Row 2 ______________________

Row 3 ______________________ Row 4 ______________________

d Write a rule for finding all of the numbers in the columns.

____

e If you continued the pattern would every number between 1 and 100 appear?

Would any number be duplicated? ______________________

You need

- Calculator

Use your calculator to complete rows 1 to 3 in each pattern. Predict then write the answers to rows 4 and 5. Check with your calculator.

a $12 \times 99 = $ ______

$23 \times 99 = $ ______

$34 \times 99 = $ ______

______ = ______

______ = ______

b $8 \times 1 + 1 = $ ______

$8 \times 12 + 2 = $ ______

$8 \times 123 + 3 = $ ______

______ = ______

______ = ______

3 consecutive numbers

You need

- Calculator

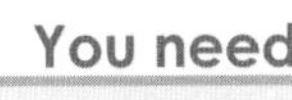

Example

14, 15, 16
$15 \times 15 = 225$
$14 \times 16 = 224$
1

Rule

- Take any 3 consecutive numbers and square the middle number.
- Multiply the outside numbers.
- Find the difference between the products.

a Use your calculator to test six different sets of 2-digit consecutive numbers. What do you notice?

b Check if the rule will work for these sets of 3-digit consecutive numbers.

135, 136, 137 268, 269, 270 901, 902, 903

c This pattern of numbers is called the Fibonacci sequence

1, 1, 2, 3, 5, 8, 13, 21, 34, 55, ____, ____, ...

- Work out the next two numbers in the sequence.
- Will the rule apply to numbers in the Fibonacci sequence? Write what you find out.

Go and find!

1 Go online and find out about the Enigma machine and how Allied mathematicians, stationed at Bletchley Park during World War II were able to decipher German military communications.

2 Go online and look up Leonardo Pisano, also known as Fibonacci.

Check up tasks

Ask your child: *Which of the codes was the key to solving the times tables problem?*

Ask your child: *What did you find out when you applied the rule to your sets of 2-digit consecutive numbers?*

Common factors and multiples

Top Tip for Parents

Some children may struggle to find all the factors for a number so the best way for you to approach this is to suggest that making an organised list of the factor pairs for a number is a sensible approach.

Example The pairs of factors for 24 are: (1, 24), (2, 12), (3, 8), (4, 6), (6, 4), (8, 3), (12, 2), (24, 1). Cross out the duplicates and the remaining numbers are the factors of 24, e.g. 1, 2, 3, 4, 6, 8, 12 and 24.

Multiples of any number can be divided exactly by that number, e.g.
multiples of 2: 2,4,6,8,10,12
multiples of 3: 3,6,9,12.
6, 12, 18 and 24 are **common multiples** of 2 and 3.

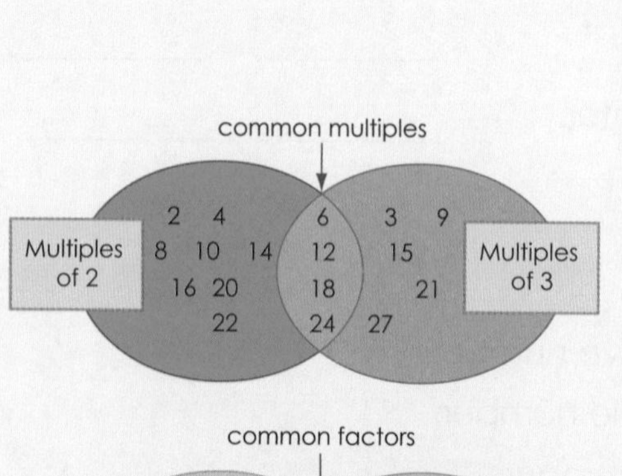

A **factor** is a whole number that divides exactly into another whole number.
The diagram shows that 1, 2, 3 and 6 are **common factors** of 18 and 30.

Exercises

1 Write the first 10 multiples of 3, 4 and 5 in the table.

Multiples of 3	3	6	9							
Multiples of 4										
Multiples of 5										

2 Look at your answer to question 1. Write two common multiples of:

a 3 and 4 ________ b 3 and 5 ________ c 4 and 5 ________

3 Find the next five common multiples of:

a 3 and 4 ________ b 3 and 5 ________ c 4 and 5 ________

4 Find the lowest common multiple of:

a 2, 3 and 8 ☐ b 3, 4 and 6 ☐ c 2, 6 and 9 ☐

d 2, 3 and 7 ☐ e 4, 6 and 9 ☐ f 4, 5, 6 and 10 ☐

List the factors of each number in a systematic way.

a Factors of 40 b Factors of 64 c Factors of 90

Example

Factors of 24
1 × 24, 2 × 12
3 × 8, 4 × 6

a Record the factors for the numbers in this table.

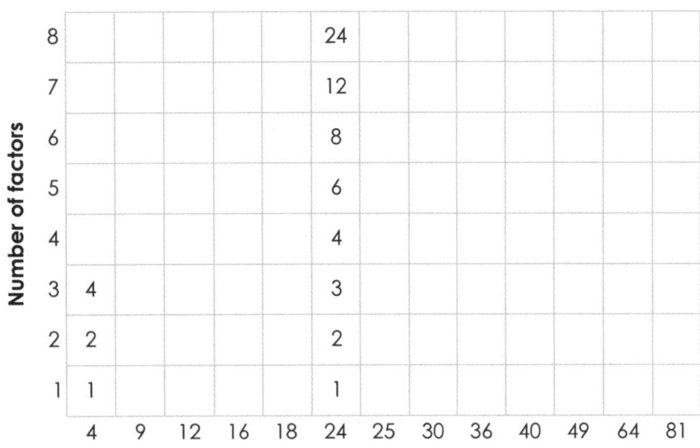

Number of factors													
8						24							
7						12							
6						8							
5						6							
4						4							
3	4					3							
2	2					2							
1	1					1							
	4	9	12	16	18	24	25	30	36	40	49	64	81

b From the table, list the numbers which have:

i an even number of factors ______________________

ii an odd number of factors ______________________

c What are the numbers listed in b ii called? ______________________

GO! Go and do!

1 **Factor game** **An activity for two players**

- Each player places a coin on a number and records the factors for their number.
- The player who finds more factors wins both coins.
- If the number of factors is the same, both players keep their coins.
- The numbers used are now crossed out.
- Continue with different numbers until one player has won all eight coins.

You need

- 1–100 number square (download from web)
- 4 coins per player
- Pencil and paper

1	2	3	4	5	6	7	8	9	10
11	12	13	14	15	16	17	18	19	20
21	22	23	24	25	26	27	28	29	30
31	32	33	34	35	36	37			

Check up tasks

Ask your child: *Tell me a multiple of 7 greater than 50. What are the first 5 common multiples of 3 and 7? Tell me all the pairs of factors of 30. What are the factors of 32? What kind of number has an odd number of factors?*

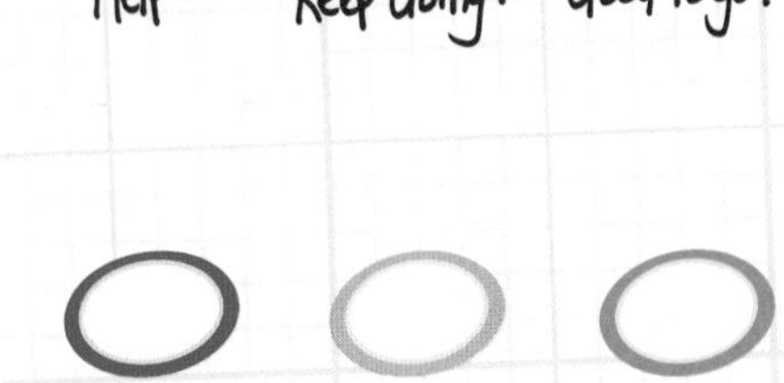

Negative differences

Numbers can be positive or negative.
Positive numbers are greater than zero.
Negative numbers are less than zero.
We read negative numbers as:
negative 1, negative 2 ... and so on.

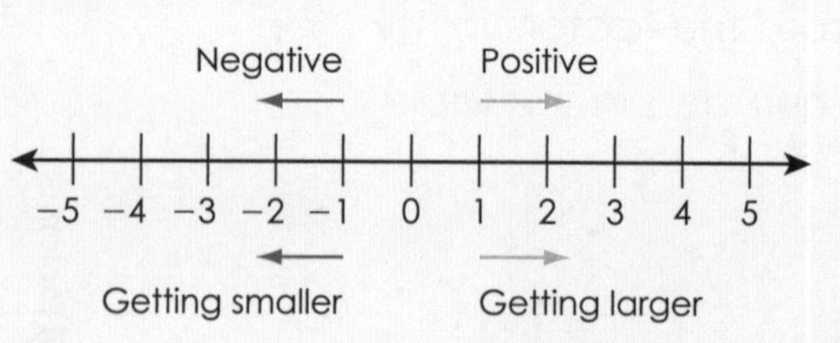

Example:

−5 is smaller than −2   2 is larger than −4

When we refer to negative numbers in the context of temperature we say: minus 1, minus 2 ... and so on.

Example:

Temperatures in Aberdeen

At 8:00 am −5°C

At 2:00 pm +4°C

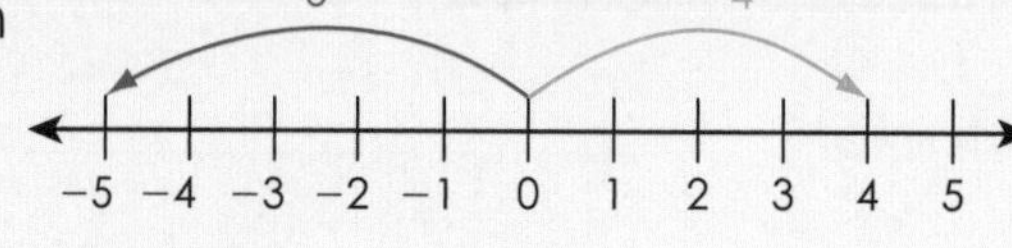

The difference between −5°C and +4°C is 9°C.

The temperature rose by 9 degrees.

Top Tip for Parents

Remind your child that subtraction can be thought of as the difference between two numbers, or what must be added to the second number to make the first. A number line can help your child to make the calculation.

Exercises

1 Write two numbers with a difference of 5 in each box. At least one of the numbers must be a negative number.

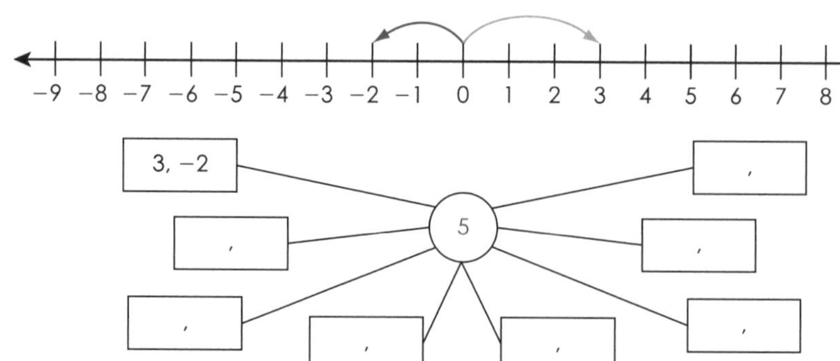

2 These temperatures were recorded at Edinburgh Airport in December.
Complete the table. *Use the number line in question 1 to help you.*

Temperature in °C	Sun	Mon	Tues	Wed	Thur	Fri	Sat
Maximum temperature	3°	0°	−2°		4°	1°	5°
Minimum temperature	−4°	−9°		−13°	−6°		−1°
Difference	7°		8°	10°		6°	

Complete these magic squares.

Remember: all the rows, columns and diagonals have the same total.

a

−2		−4	
	−5		
		−8	−15

b

	−10	−5	
	−8		
	−6		−24

c

	0	4	−7	
−5	2	−2		
	3			
8		1		2

d

0		7	−6	
4	−3			
	8	2		
5			3	2

Go and do!

You need
- Playing cards

1 **Order the cards** **An activity for one player**

- Remove the aces, kings, queens and jacks from the pack of cards. Shuffle the remaining cards. Place them face down in a pile.
- The red cards, ♥ and ♦, are negative numbers. The black cards, ♣ and ♠, are positive numbers.
- Turn over six cards and place them in the order in which they came from the pack.
- Swap the position of two cards at a time until all six cards are in order from smallest to largest.
- After several rounds with six cards, move on to using eight or ten cards.

Example

6♥	4♠	5♦	10♣	8♠	8♥
6♥	8♥	5♦	10♣	8♠	4♠
8♥	6♥	5♦	10♣	8♠	4♠
8♥	6♥	5♦	4♠	8♠	10♠

2 **On the cards** **An activity for two players**

You need
- Playing cards

- Use the same set of cards as in **Order the cards.**
- Each player takes two cards, finds the difference between their two numbers and records this in the grid. The player with the greater difference wins 1 point.

Examples: 6♥ and 4♠. Difference = 10. 8♦ and 4♥. Difference = 4.

Player 1							
Player 2							

Go and find!

Go to the website: http://www.metoffice.gov.uk. Click on UK weather. Next click on Climate, then on Weather extremes. Investigate the monthly temperature records for Scotland.

Check up tasks

Ask your child: *I am thinking of two numbers with a difference of 6. One of the numbers is a negative 4. What is my number?*

Ask your child: *What will the temperature be if it is now 4°C and falls by 9°C?*

Simply fractions

When we simplify a fraction we reduce it to its lowest terms, i.e. to the smallest numbers we can. We need to find a number that will divide exactly into both the top number (the numerator) and the bottom number (the denominator). For example, in the fraction $\frac{2}{10}$, we can divide (or cancel) by 2 so $\frac{2}{10} = \frac{1}{5}$. The value of the fraction has not been changed because both the numerator and the denominator have been divided by 2. Thus $\frac{2}{10}$ and $\frac{1}{5}$ are equivalent fractions.

Top Tip for Parents

If your child struggles with the idea of equivalent fractions you might like to try this. Lay out 10 sweets. Take away 2 sweets. Agree that you have taken 2 out of the 10 or $\frac{2}{10}$ of the sweets. Now put the sweets into 5 sets of 2. Take 1 set of sweets. Agree that you have taken 1 out of 5 or $\frac{1}{5}$ of the sweets and that each time the answer is 2 sweets.

Exercises

1 In the multiplication square the top two rows show the multiples of 1 and 2.
Together they show the nine fractions equivalent to $\frac{1}{2}$.

$\frac{1}{2} = \frac{2}{4}, \frac{3}{6}, \frac{4}{8}, \frac{5}{10}, \frac{6}{12}, \frac{7}{14}, \frac{8}{16}, \frac{9}{18}$, and $\frac{10}{20}$

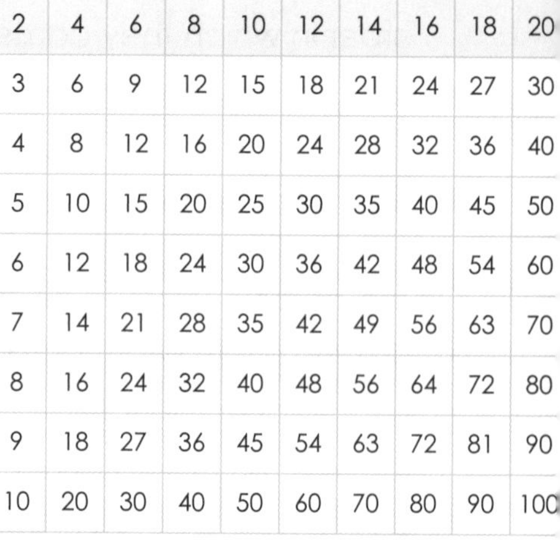

1	2	3	4	5	6	7	8	9	10
2	4	6	8	10	12	14	16	18	20
3	6	9	12	15	18	21	24	27	30
4	8	12	16	20	24	28	32	36	40
5	10	15	20	25	30	35	40	45	50
6	12	18	24	30	36	42	48	54	60
7	14	21	28	35	42	49	56	63	70
8	16	24	32	40	48	56	64	72	80
9	18	27	36	45	54	63	72	81	90
10	20	30	40	50	60	70	80	90	100

a Find two rows from the grid to make nine fractions equivalent to:

i $\frac{1}{5} =$

ii $\frac{1}{3} =$

b Write five fractions that are equivalent to:

i $\frac{3}{7} =$ ii $\frac{2}{5} =$

iii $\frac{4}{9} =$ iv $\frac{5}{8} =$

c Use the grid to reduce each fraction to its simplest form.

i $\frac{10}{35} =$ ii $\frac{18}{36} =$ iii $\frac{30}{40} =$ iv $\frac{27}{72} =$

v $\frac{15}{45} =$ vi $\frac{18}{60} =$ vii $\frac{28}{56} =$ viii $\frac{42}{63} =$

Example

$\frac{\cancel{12}^{2}}{\cancel{36}_{6}} = \frac{\cancel{2}^{1}}{\cancel{6}_{3}} = \frac{1}{3}$

2 Find the fraction of each shape that is: (i) red, (ii) not red.

a

i = ____ ii = ____

b

i = ____ ii = ____

c

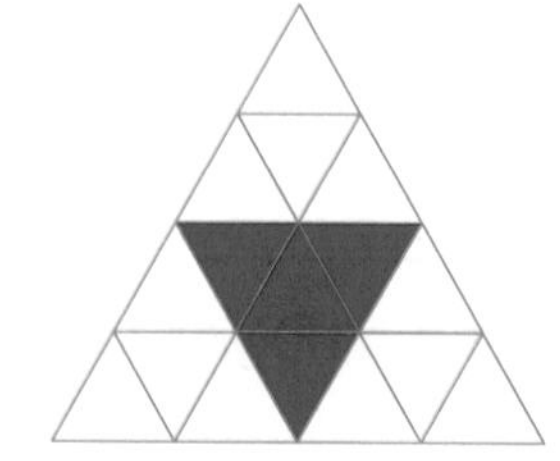

i = ____ ii = ____

d

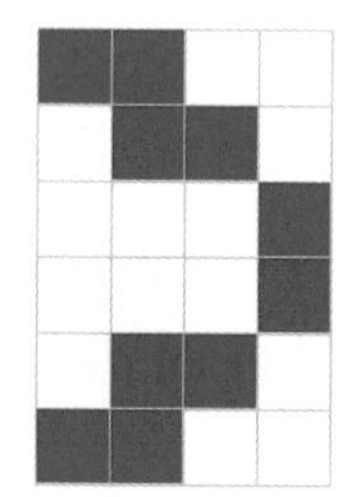

i = ____ ii = ____

Convert these fractions to equivalent fractions, then order them from smallest to largest.

Example

I know 2 and 3 go into 6. $\frac{5}{6}, \frac{2}{3}, \frac{1}{2}$

$\frac{1}{2} = \frac{3}{6}$

$\frac{2}{3} = \frac{4}{6}$

Order: $\frac{1}{2}, \frac{2}{3}, \frac{5}{6}$

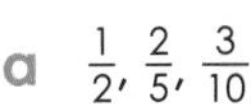

a $\frac{1}{2}, \frac{2}{5}, \frac{3}{10}$ Order ____________

b $\frac{5}{16}, \frac{1}{4}, \frac{3}{8}$ Order ____________

c $\frac{2}{5}, \frac{7}{10}, \frac{9}{20}$ Order ____________

d $\frac{3}{5}, \frac{5}{6}, \frac{7}{10}$ Order ____________

e $\frac{7}{8}, \frac{5}{6}, \frac{11}{12}$ Order ____________

f $\frac{3}{4}, \frac{1}{2}, \frac{2}{3}, \frac{5}{8}$ Order ____________

g $\frac{3}{4}, \frac{7}{9}, \frac{5}{6}, \frac{1}{2}$ Order ____________

Go and do!

You need
- 1 cm squared paper
- Scissors
- Ruler

1 *You can cut a 4 × 4 square in half in 12 different ways.*
True or false? Investigate.
Here are three ways you can do it.

a
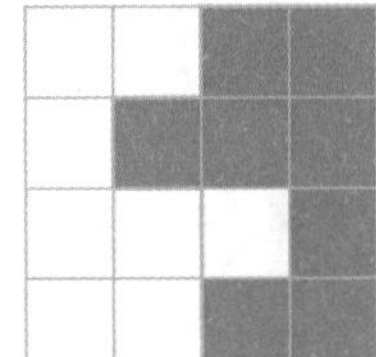

b
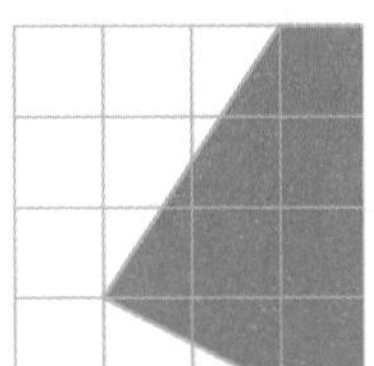

c
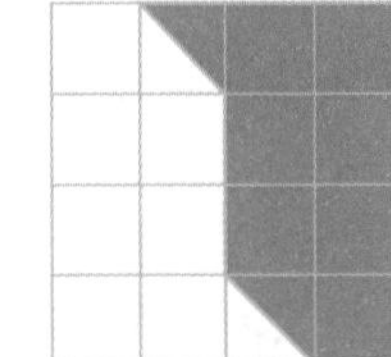

2 **All in order** **A game for two players**

You need
- 1–10 number cards.

- Shuffle and deal 4 cards to each player.
- Make six different fractions with your cards.
- Write your fractions in order, smallest to largest.

Scoring

2 points 6 fractions in order

1 point 1 fraction out of order.

Example

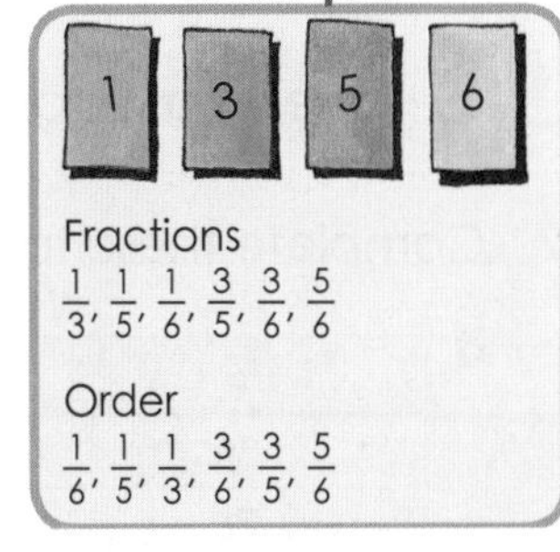

Fractions
$\frac{1}{3}, \frac{1}{5}, \frac{1}{6}, \frac{3}{5}, \frac{3}{6}, \frac{5}{6}$

Order
$\frac{1}{6}, \frac{1}{5}, \frac{1}{3}, \frac{3}{6}, \frac{3}{5}, \frac{5}{6}$

3 **Equivalent fractions**
Choose two numbers. Make the smaller number the numerator and the larger number the denominator. Make as many fractions as you can which are equivalent to $\frac{1}{2}$, $\frac{2}{3}$, and $\frac{3}{4}$.

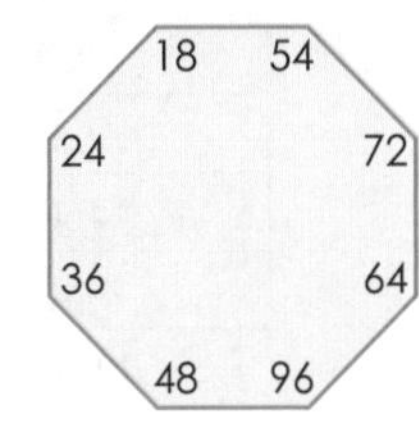

Check up tasks

Ask your child: *In Question 1a of Go and Do! half of the squares are shaded. How many squares would you shade to find $\frac{1}{4}$, $\frac{1}{8}$, $\frac{3}{4}$, $\frac{7}{8}$ of the rectangle? Which is the greater fraction, $\frac{3}{4}$ or $\frac{7}{8}$? How do you know?*

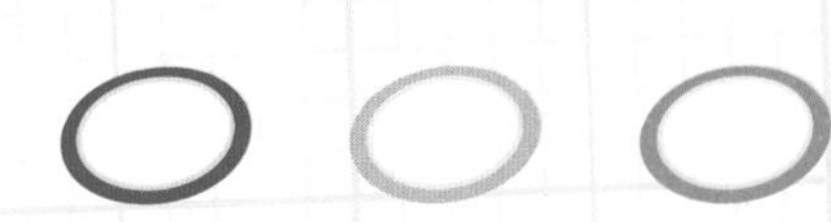

Finding percentages

A percentage is the number of parts in every 100. The sign for per cent is %. Imagine you took a test that was worth 100 marks. If you scored 100% it would mean that you made no errors at all. A score of 97% would mean '97 out of 100' or 97/100 and you lost three marks.

Top Tip for Parents

Check that your child knows by heart the percentage equivalences of simple fractions e.g. $\frac{1}{4}$, $\frac{1}{5}$, $\frac{1}{10}$. Remind your child that when finding 20% of an amount it is sometimes easier to find 10% and double the answer than to divide the amount by 5.

Exercises

You need

- Coloured pens or pencils

1 a In this 100-square, cross out:
multiples of 2 in red;
multiples of 3 in blue;
and multiples of 5 in green.

1	2	3	4	5	6	7	8	9	10
11	12	13	14	15	16	17	18	19	20
21	22	23	24	25	26	27	28	29	30
31	32	33	34	35	36	37	38	39	40
41	42	43	44	45	46	47	48	49	50
51	52	53	54	55	56	57	58	59	60
61	62	63	64	65	66	67	68	69	70
71	72	73	74	75	76	77	78	79	80
81	82	83	84	85	86	87	88	89	90
91	92	93	94	95	96	97	98	99	100

b Now complete the table.

Multiple	No. of squares with a cross	% of squares with a cross
2		
3		
5		

c Write as a percentage the number of squares not crossed out. ______ %

2 Complete these tables.

a

Amount	50%	25%	75%
36	18	9	27
76			
180			
220			
460			
940			
1120			

b

Amount	10%	20%	5%	30%
£72	£7·20	£14·40	£3·60	£21·60
£25				
£66				
£84				
£160				
£350				
£1200				

Go and do!

1 100 per cent **A game for two or more players**

You need
- 1–9 number cards
- Calculator

- Shuffle the cards. On your turn, take the top card, e.g. 7. Multiply 7 by 10 to create the percentage 70%.
- Choose a number from the box, e.g. 420.
- Without using a calculator, work out the answer, e.g. 70% of 420 = 294.
- Your partner checks your answer by pressing these calculator keys: 4 2 0 × 7 0 %
- If your answer of 294 is correct, add the digits, e.g. 2 + 9 + 4 = 15. This is your score for that round.
- The first player to score 100 points is the winner.

150	**940**	**450**
850	**270**	**530**
360	**730**	**620**
420	**690**	**810**
510	**180**	**390**

2 Bouncing balls

You need
- Calculator

When a ball is dropped from the top of a 50 m tower it bounces back up to a height equal to 40% of the height of the tower. The ball continues to bounce. Each time it rises to a height which is 40% of its previous bounce.

a To what height will the ball rise after 4 bounces? ______ m

b After which bounce will the ball rise less than 0·5 m? ______ th bounce.

Go and find!

1 Go online to en.wikipedia.org and search for the tallest building in the world.

a Name the building. Give its height in metres. ______________
Imagine dropping the ball from the top of this building!

b To what height will the ball rise after 4 bounces? ______ m

c After which bounce will the ball rise less than1 m? ______ th bounce.

2 Cut a length of string 50 cm long. Cut the string in two. Measure one of the pieces of string to the nearest millimetre. What percentage of 50 cm is it? What percentage of the whole length is the second length?
Repeat as above by cutting the string to different lengths.

Check up tasks

Ask your child: *What is 20% of 60? How did you work it out? What is 5% of 60? How would you go about finding 75% of £120?*

What's the equivalence?

> **Top Tip for Parents**
>
> Remind your child that there are two ways to convert a fraction to a decimal:
> - To find the equivalent decimal for $\frac{4}{5}$, first find $\frac{1}{5}$ $(1 \div 5 = 0{\cdot}2)$ and multiply the answer by 4 $(0{\cdot}2 \times 4 = 0{\cdot}8)$ so $\frac{4}{5} = 0{\cdot}8$
> - The quick way is: $\frac{4}{5} = \frac{8}{10} = 0{\cdot}8$

Equivalent means of equal value. Things which are equivalent to each other are worth the same. Fractions, decimals and percentages can be equivalent to each other, e.g.

$\frac{1}{2} = \frac{5}{10}$ or $\frac{50}{100}$ $\qquad$ $\frac{5}{10}$ or $\frac{50}{100} = 0{\cdot}5$ $\qquad$ $\frac{50}{100}$ or $0{\cdot}5 = 50\%$

It is useful to learn these fractions as decimals and percentages as we often need them.

$\frac{1}{10} = \frac{10}{100} = 0{\cdot}1 = 10\%$ $\qquad$ $\frac{1}{5} = \frac{20}{100} = 0{\cdot}2 = 20\%$ $\qquad$ $\frac{1}{20} = \frac{5}{100} = 0{\cdot}05 = 5\%$

$\frac{1}{2} = \frac{50}{100} = 0{\cdot}5 = 50\%$ $\qquad$ $\frac{1}{4} = \frac{25}{100} = 0{\cdot}25 = 25\%$ $\qquad$ $\frac{3}{4} = \frac{75}{100} = 0{\cdot}75 = 75\%$

$\frac{1}{8} = \frac{125}{1000} = 0{\cdot}125 = 12\frac{1}{2}\%$ $\qquad$ $\frac{1}{3} \approx 0{\cdot}333 = 33\frac{1}{3}\%$ $\qquad$ $\frac{2}{3} \approx 0{\cdot}667 = 66\frac{2}{3}\%$

Exercises

1 Find the missing equivalents and complete the table.

Fraction	$\frac{4}{5}$			$\frac{3}{4}$			$\frac{11}{20}$
Decimal	0·8	0·7			0·375		
Percentage	80%		40%			$66\frac{2}{3}\%$	

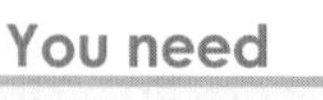

You need

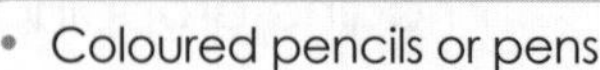

- Coloured pencils or pens

2 Colour each grid as directed. Then find the percentage of the square that is white.

a $\frac{1}{4}$ red
$\frac{1}{5}$ blue
25% green
% white = ______%

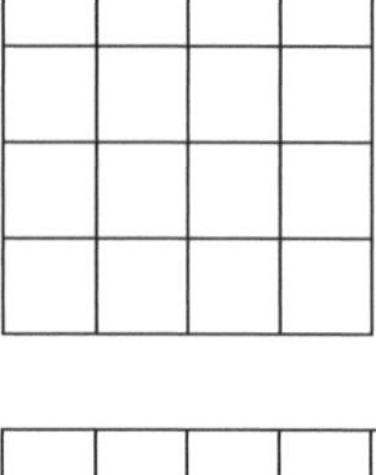

b $\frac{1}{10}$ blue
$\frac{3}{10}$ green
20% yellow
% white = ______%

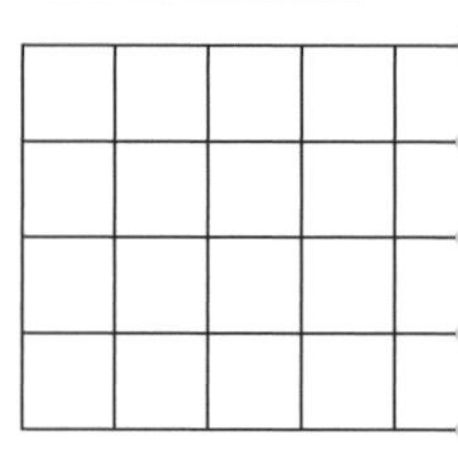

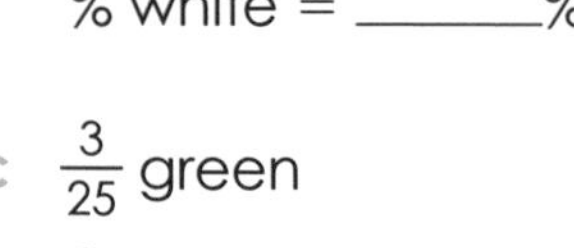

c $\frac{3}{25}$ green
$\frac{2}{5}$ yellow
20% red
% white = ______%

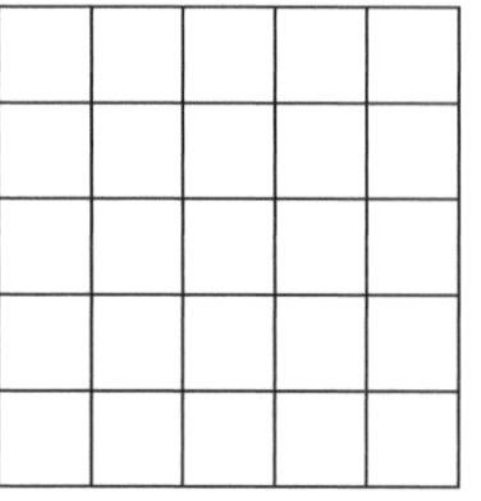

d $\frac{1}{8}$ yellow
$\frac{1}{4}$ red
50% blue
% white = ______%

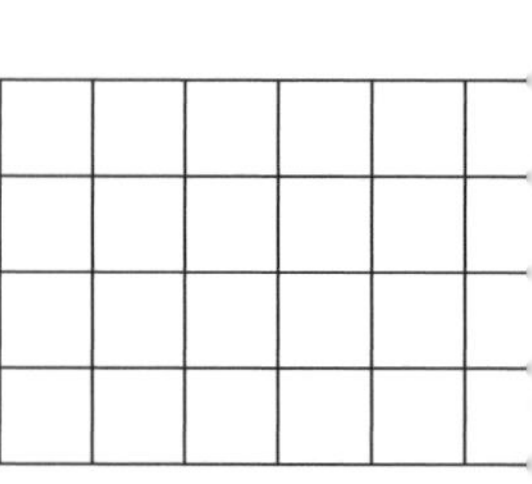

A 5p coin is worth $\frac{1}{2}$ or 0·5 or 50% of a 10p coin.

a Find the equivalent value of a 5p coin to these coins and complete the table.

5p coin	10p coin	20p coin	50p coin	£1 coin	£2 coin
Fraction	$\frac{1}{2}$				
Decimal	0·5				
Percentage	50%				

b Now find the equivalent value of a 2p coin to these coins.

2p coin	5p coin	10p coin	20p coin	50p coin	£1 coin	£2 coin
Fraction	$\frac{2}{5}$					
Decimal	0·4					
Percentage	40%					

Go and do!

You need

- A set of 28 dominoes

1 **Domino descriptions**

Find how many of the 28 dominoes in the set match each description. Complete the table.

Description	Fraction	Decimal (to 2 decimal places)	Percentage (to nearest whole number)
Is a double	$\frac{7}{28} = \frac{1}{4}$		
Sum of the dots is greater than 6			
With at least one even number			
Does not have a blank			
Difference is an odd number			

2 a Match the fraction and the decimal that, when added together, equal 100%.

$\frac{1}{8}$ $\frac{21}{30}$ $\frac{6}{60}$ $\frac{9}{36}$ $\frac{2}{5}$

$\frac{14}{16}$ $\frac{36}{72}$ $\frac{23}{50}$ $\frac{18}{24}$

0·125 0·6 0·875 0·9

0·25 0·75 0·5 0·3 0·54

b Make up some more examples for a friend to answer.

Check up tasks

Ask your child: *Can you tell me how you worked out how many boxes to colour in Exercises question 2d? What percentage of a set of dominoes are not doubles?*

Fractions and percentages

Top Tip for Parents

Use a supermarket flyer or a store catalogue to give your child extra practice in finding the fraction or percentage of whole number quantities.

To find a fraction of a measure, e.g. $\frac{3}{4}$ of 22 kg, we first find the value of the unitary fraction, i.e. $\frac{1}{4}$ and then multiply the answer by 3.	$\frac{3}{4}$ of 22 kg $\frac{1}{4} = 22 \div 4 = 5{\cdot}5$ kg $\frac{3}{4} = 5{\cdot}5 \times 3 = 16{\cdot}5$ kg
To find 60% of 2ℓ in millilitres, we first convert litres to ml and find 10% and then we multiply the answer by 6.	60% of 2000 ml 10% = 2000 ÷ 10 = 200 ml 60% = 200 × 6 = 1200 ml
A quick way to find 25% of an amount, e.g. 25% of £14 is to halve the amount and then to halve it again.	100% = £14 50% of £14 = £7 25% of £14 = £3·50

Exercises

1 Find the fractions of these weights in kilograms.

a 15 kg

$\frac{3}{10}$ of 15 kg

$\frac{1}{10}$ =

$\frac{3}{10}$ =

b 25 kg

$\frac{2}{5}$ of 25 kg

$\frac{1}{5}$ =

$\frac{2}{5}$ =

c

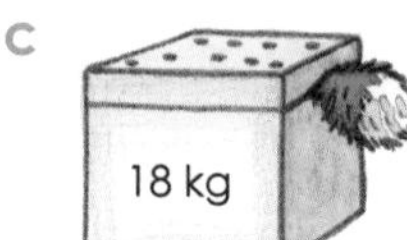

$\frac{3}{4}$ of 18 kg

$\frac{1}{4}$ =

$\frac{3}{4}$ =

d

$\frac{5}{6}$ of 21 kg

$\frac{1}{6}$ =

$\frac{5}{6}$ =

e

$\frac{7}{8}$ of 36 kg

$\frac{1}{8}$ =

$\frac{7}{8}$ =

2 Find the percentages of these capacities in millilitres.

a 500 ml

30% of 500 ml

10% =

30% =

b

40% of 1·2 ℓ

c

60% of 3 ℓ

d

5% of 2 ℓ

e

75% of 5 ℓ

Find the VAT (Valued Added Tax) at 20% and the total cost of these items.

a

Price =
VAT =
Total price =

b

£ 27

Price =
VAT =
Total price =

c

Price =
VAT =
Total price =

d

Price =
VAT =
Total price =

The sale at Sports World has everything reduced by at least 10%. For each item:

- work out the price reduction
- then write the sale price.

Example

£14

Rugby ball
10% of £14 = £1·40
Sale price = £14 − £1·40
= £12·60

a Tennis racquet 25% off

b Skis 20% off

c Hockey stick 10% off

d Football $12\frac{1}{2}$% off

e Ice skates 30% off

f Snowboard 15% off

At 10:00 a tortoise is lumbering towards the garden wall 50 m away. At 11:00 it has covered $\frac{1}{2}$ the distance towards the wall. At 12:00 it has managed $\frac{4}{5}$ of the remaining distance. What fraction of the original distance has it still to go?

Go and do!

1 **Percentage cards**

Select several 0–9 digit cards and the of, % and = cards to make as many different statements as you can.

Check your answers on your calculator.

You need

- 0–9 digit cards
- Cards for of, %, =
- Calculator

Examples:

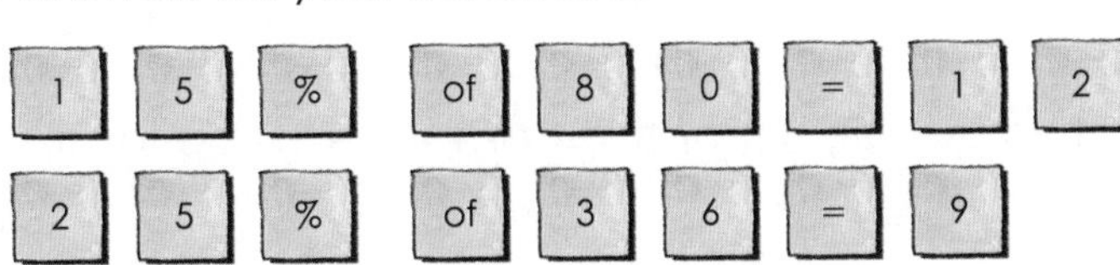

2 **In the supermarket**

Look for special offers such as *440 g for the price of 400 g* and work out what percentage is free.

Check up tasks

Ask your child: *How did you work out $\frac{7}{8}$ of 36 kg … 75% of 5 ℓ … 15% of £70?*

Manage money

In this topic we look at real-life situations which involve comparing the costs of goods, finding the best buy and using a savings plan as part of good budgeting.

Top Tip for Parents

Here are some useful strategies to find the fraction or percentage of an amount:

- $\frac{1}{8}$ – find $\frac{1}{4}$ and halve it
- 15% – find 10%, halve it to find 5% and add the answers.

Exercises

1 To promote sales, supermarkets will make displays of their special offers at the end of aisles. Depending on what is on your shopping list, it can be a good idea to check the special offe price against the shelf price for the best buy.

a Which is the better buy, the special offer or the equivalent from the supermarket shelf? Find the cost for each item and complete the table.

Shopping list	Special offer price	Cost	Shelf price	Cost
6 morning rolls	90p per pack of 6		20p each	
3 peppers	£1·50 per bag of 3		55p each	
400 g bacon	£4·95 per 400 g pack		£2·60 per 200 g pack	
12 large eggs	£1·90 per 6 box		£3·25 per 12 box	
4 cans beans	£1·00 per pack of 4		29p each	
240 tea bags	£1·29 per box of 80		£3·45 per box of 240	

b Choose the better buy for each item and complete the table.

Shopping list	Cost	Saving
6 morning rolls		
3 peppers		
400 g bacon		
12 large eggs		
4 cans beans		
240 tea bags		
Total		

2 You compare the prices for two equally attractive campsites in Scotland.

Castle Bay £6·50 per night

Lochside Park £45 per week

You want to stay for 14 nights in July.

Which campsite offers the better rates? ____________________

Work out the sale price of each item.

a

Sale price = £

b

Sale price = £

c

Sale price = £

d

Sale price = £

e

Sale price = £

f

Sale price = £

g

Sale price = £

h

Sale price = £

i

Sale price = £

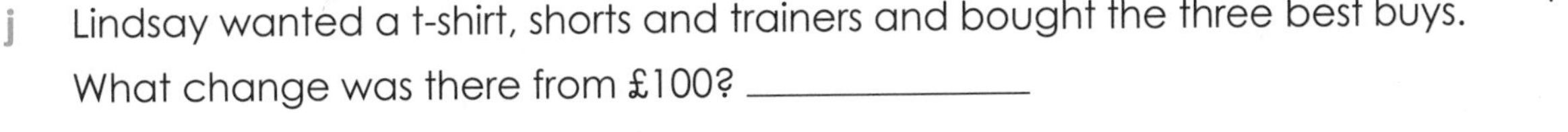

j Lindsay wanted a t-shirt, shorts and trainers and bought the three best buys.
What change was there from £100? ____________

4 A savings plan is part of good budgeting. These children drew up a savings plan in January. Work out in which month they will reach their savings goal.

Savings plan	Simon	Amy	Vera	Eddie
I'd like to save	£100	£60	£150	£75
I have already saved	£42	£15	£85	£29
Each month I can save	£10	£5	£8	£4
I will reach my savings goal in				

Go and find!

Make your own savings plan by visiting the site www.lloydstsb.com and click on Budgeting Help.

Check up tasks

Ask your child: *Look at the t-shirts in question 3. Which t-shirt would be the best buy if all three t-shirts were reduced by 25%?*

Profit and loss

Top Tip for Parents

Remind your child that it is sometimes easier to calculate a percentage if you use the equivalent fraction.

You make a profit when the money you receive from a transaction or an investment is more than your initial outlay. When the money you receive is less, you make a loss.

Exercises

1 50% of the money a cinema takes in from the sales of refreshments is profit. The pie chart shows percentages of refreshments sold in one day. If the cinema takes £500 in refreshment sales, work out the profit for each type of refreshment.

Refreshments sold (%)

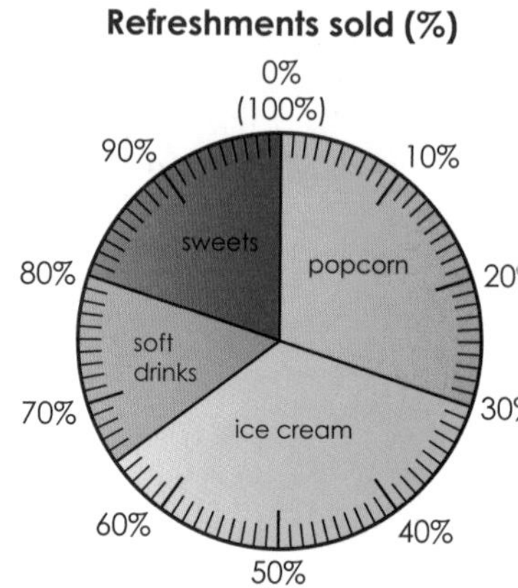

Type of refreshment	Percentage of refreshment	Profit
Popcorn		
Soft drinks		
Ice cream		
Sweets		

2 Pupils made these goods for sale at the school fair. After deducting the cost to bake or to produce the finished item, how much profit did each child make?

Alex
24 scones
Cost to bake £2·40
Selling price 25p
Income =
=
Less cost =
Profit =

Beth
40 chocolate crispies
Cost to bake £1·75
Selling price 20p
Income =
=
Less cost =
Profit =

Example
15 cup cakes
Cost to bake £2·00
Selling price 40p
Income = 15 × £0·40
= £6·00
Less cost = £6·00 − £2·00
Profit = £4·00

Colin
30 fruit slices
Cost to bake £2·60
Selling price 30p
Income =
=
Less cost =
Profit =

Diana
50 petunia plug plants
Cost for seeds, pots and compost £5·00
Selling price 49p
Income =
=
Less cost =
Profit =

Emma and Frank
100 tickets for Lucky Dip
Cost of prizes £4·65
Selling price 4 for £1
Income =
=
Less cost =
Profit =

3 These people invested in cash ISA accounts at their local bank. The interest rate shows what they will have added to their account at the end of one year. How much were their investments worth after one year? Complete the table.

Use the row, Value after 1 year, for your workings out.

Example

£2000 at 2%
$1\% = \frac{1}{100}$ of £2000 = £20
2% = £20 × 2 = £40

	Josef	Kim	Len	Marie	Nafisa
Amount invested	£4000	£3000	£5000	£2000	£2500
Interest rate	2%	4%	3%	$2\frac{1}{2}$%	5%
Profit					
Value after 1 year					

4 These people each bought £1000 worth of shares. What was the value of their shares after six months of trading on the Stock Exchange?

Example

Investment = £1000
Profit of 20% = £200
Value = £1200

a Mark

I made a 10% profit
Value =

b Mitch

I made a 10% loss
Value =

c May

I made a 50% profit
Value =

d Molly

I made a 30% loss
Value =

e Megan

I made a 25% profit
Value =

f Martin

I made a 15% loss
Value =

g Maya

I made a 65% profit
Value =

Go and do!

Imagine you have £200 to put into a savings account. Investigate the best rate of interest you could earn if you left the money in the account for one year. If you left the money there for three years the interest would earn interest as well. How much money would you have at the end of three years?

Check up tasks

Ask your child: *How did you work out the profit for Emma and Frank? Suppose Mark had invested £5000 instead of £1000, what is the new value of his shares?*

Times and events

Most timetables use the 24-hour clock. Airline timetables show 9:30 am as 09:30 and 9:30 pm as 21:30. Train and ferry timetables omit the colon, e.g. 0930 and 2130.

Exercises

1 British Airways operates seven weekday flights from London Heathrow to Aberdeen. The flight time is 1 hour and 30 minutes.

a Complete the timetable.

Depart Heathrow	07:15	08:55		14:20			20:20
Arrive Aberdeen	08:45		13:20		17:35	19:50	

b The departure of the 14:20 flight is delayed by 15 minutes. What are the new departure and arrival times? Depart _______ Arrive _______

c Mr MacIntyre's flight from Houston was late in arriving at Heathrow and he missed his 08:55 connection to Aberdeen. How long had he to wait for the next flight to Aberdeen? ____________________

2 This is part of the train timetable from Edinburgh to Glasgow Queen Street.

Edinburgh	0730	0745	v	0800
Haymarket	0734	0749	v	0804
Linlithgow	0748	0803	0759[B]	v
Polmont	0755	v	v	0822
Falkirk High	0800	0812	0811[f]	0826
Croy	0810	v	v	0836
Lenzie	v	0825	0832	v
Bishopbriggs	v	v	0836	v
Glasgow	0825	0840	0847	0855

Key:

V train does not stop here

B From Kirkcaldy dep. 0714

f Falkirk Grahamston Station

a How long is the journey from Edinburgh to Glasgow?

b Mr Martin misses the 0755 train at Polmont by 2 minutes. How long must he wait for the next train?

c Alan lives in Linlithgow. His first lecture at Strathclyde University, a 10-minute walk from Queen Street, is at 9 am. Which train should he catch?

d Sarah lives near Haymarket and works in Bishopbriggs. If she takes the 0734 train, at which station should she get off to connect with the 0714 from Kirkcaldy? What if she takes the 0749 train?

The Bute Highland Games are held in Rothesay every August. The timetable shows the rail and ferry connections to the island.

a Kirsty is a Highland dancer. Which train from Glasgow should she and her family take to arrive in Rothesay before 12 noon? ______

b Calum is a piper with Milngavie Pipe Band. The coach carrying the band is booked on the 10:15 ferry and has to arrive at Wemyss Bay at least 30 minutes before the ferry sails. Go to the website www.aa-route-planner.co.uk. Find the travelling time from Milngavie to Wemyss Bay. When should the coach leave Milngavie? ______

BUTE

WEMYSS BAY – ROTHESAY

TEXT CODE 03	Glasgow Central	Wemyss Bay	WEMYSS BAY	ROTHESAY
	Depart	Arrive	Depart	Arrive
MON – SAT	0605	0658	0715 A	0750 A
	0632	0730	0800	0835
	0750	0840	0845	0920
	–	–	0925	1000
	0850	0940	1015	1050
	0950	1040	1100	1135
	1050	1140	1200	1235
	1150	1240	1305	1340
	1250	1340	1405	1440
	1350	1440	1500	1535
	1450	1540	1600	1635

c The 10 k run via Ardbeg starts and finishes at the King George V Park. An Inverclyde Sports Club entered three teams. The race began at 2:30 pm.

i Fill in the missing details.

	Red Team			Blue Team		
	1 Alex	2 Ben	3 Kim	1 Derek	2 Flo	3 Pat
Start time	2:30 pm	2:30 pm	2:30 pm	2:30 pm	2:30 pm	2:30 pm
Running time	50 min		62 min		47 min	
Finishing time		3:25 pm		3:28 pm		3:34 pm

ii What was the overall time for the Red Team? ______ The Blue Team? ______

iii The Green Team's overall time was 2 hr 45 min. Work out the times for:

Runner 1: 4 □ min Runner 2: 52 min Runner 3: □ 5 min.

Go and do!

You need
- A watch with a seconds hand

1 **TV Research**
Choose an hour's TV viewing on a non-BBC channel. Record in minutes and seconds the amount of time given over to TV adverts. Find the percentage of time taken up by adverts in a 60 minute period of viewing.

2 How many different times will the digits 0, 1, 2 and 3 appear together on a digital clock face? List the times in order beginning at 01:23.

Check up tasks

Ask your child: *You are on the 07:45 train from Edinburgh to Glasgow. Where are you on your journey at 4 minutes to 8? How long is the ferry crossing from Wemyss Bay to Rothesay?*

Help! Keep Going! Good to go!

Time, speed and distance

Top Tip for Parents

Your child may find it helpful to visualise the situations in question 3.

To calculate the **time** taken to travel a distance we need to know: • the distance it travels; • the speed at which the object moved.	A car travels 280 km at 80 km/h. It will travel 80 km in 1 hour. Time = 280 ÷ 80 hrs = 3·5 hrs This gives us the formula: T = D ÷ S.
Speed tells us how fast an object is moving. To calculate an object's speed we need to know: • the distance it travels; • the time taken to travel this distance.	A car travels 100 km in 2 hours. It will travel 50 km in 1 hour. Speed = 100 ÷ 2 km/h = 50 km/h This gives us the formula: S = D ÷ T.
To calculate the **distance** travelled we need to know: • the speed at which the object moved; • the time taken to travel the distance.	A car travels at 70 mph for 3 hours. It will travel 70 miles in 1 hour. Distance = 70 x 3 miles = 210 miles This gives us the formula: D = S × T.

Exercises

1 Find the time each motorcyclist took to travel to 'T in the Park' at these speeds.

a 60 miles at 40 mph

T = D ÷ S

= 60 ÷ 40 hrs

= _______ hours

b 90 miles at 45 mph

c 180 miles at 60 mph

d 225 miles at 50 mph

Calculate the speed in kilometres per hour (km/h)

a

180 km in 3 hours

S = D ÷ T

= 180 ÷ 3

=

b 

250 km in 5 hours

c 

2000 km in 4 hours

d 

15 km in $\frac{1}{4}$ hour

Find the distance travelled in miles.

a bus
30 mph for 4 hours
D =

b plane
500 mph for 7 hours
D =

c lorry
60 mph for $3\frac{1}{2}$ hours
D =

d bicycle
12 mph for 20 min
D =

a How far is it from:

i home to Sports Centre? _______ miles

ii Sports Centre to Gran's house? _______ miles

iii Gran's house to home? _______ miles

b How long did Amy spend:

i at the Sports Centre? _______ hours

ii at Gran's house? _______ minutes

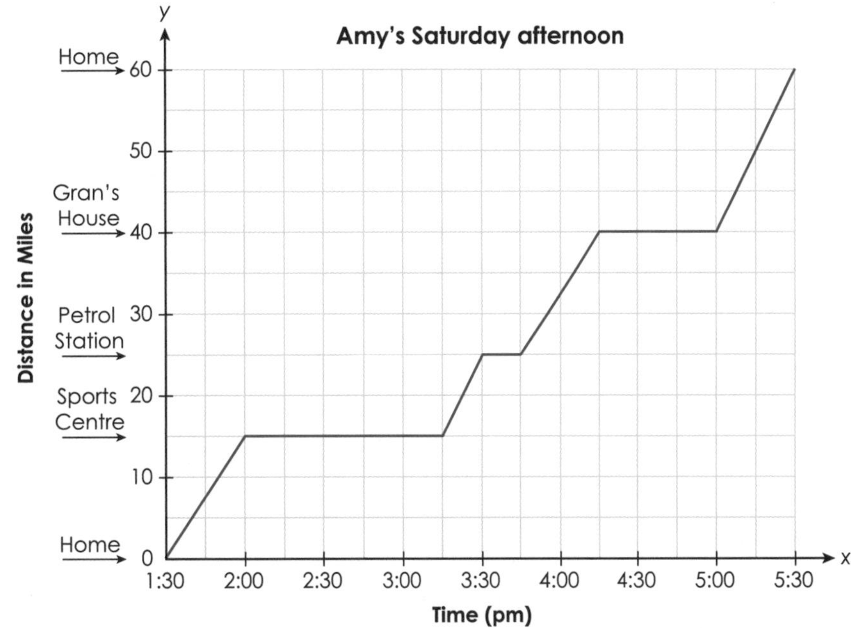

c If Amy's mum had not stopped for petrol, when would they have arrived at Gran's house? __________

Go and do!

Make up a distance–time graph like Amy's to show how you spend part of your Saturday morning or afternoon.

Check up tasks

Ask your child: *In question 2, which was faster, the car or the bus? Tell me another fact you can interpret from the graph in question 4.*

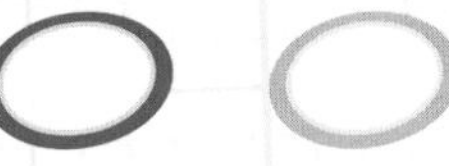

Units of measurement

Measure facts

Length	Mass	Capacity
1 km = 1000 m = 100 000 cm	**1 kg** = 1000 g	**1 ℓ** = 1000 ml
0·1 km = 100 m = 10 000 cm	0·1 kg = 100 g	0·1 ℓ = 100 ml
0·01 km = 10 m = 1000 cm	0·01 kg = 10 g	0·01 ℓ = 10 ml
1 m = 100 cm = 1000 mm	0·001 kg = 1 g	0·001 ℓ = 1 ml
0·1 m = 10 cm = 100 mm		1 cl = 10 ml
0·01 m = 1 cm = 10 mm		
1 cm = 10 mm		
0·1 cm = 1 mm		

Top Tip for Parents

Check that your child interprets the intervals on the scale correctly, e.g. on the measuring cylinder there are 10 intervals between each multiple of 100 ml so each interval is 10 ml.

Exercises

1 Complete the table to show the length of the lines drawn from zero to A, B, C, D, E and F in centimetres, in millimetres and in metres.

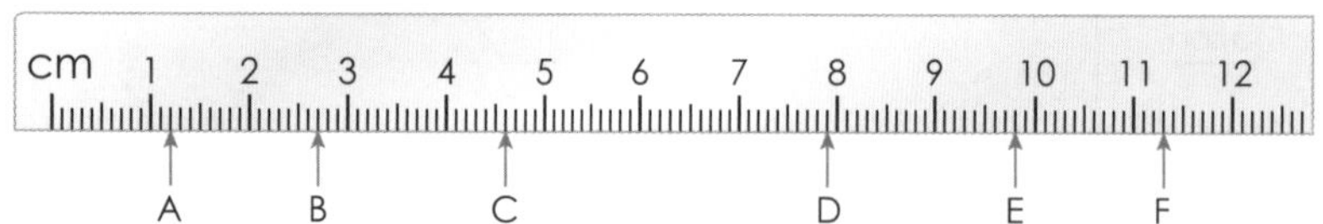

Line	Length in cm	Length in mm	Length in m
Zero to A	1·2 cm	12 mm	0·012 m
Zero to B			
Zero to C			
Zero to D			
Zero to E			
Zero to F			

2 Write the weight shown on these scales in grams and to the nearest $\frac{1}{10}$ of a kg.

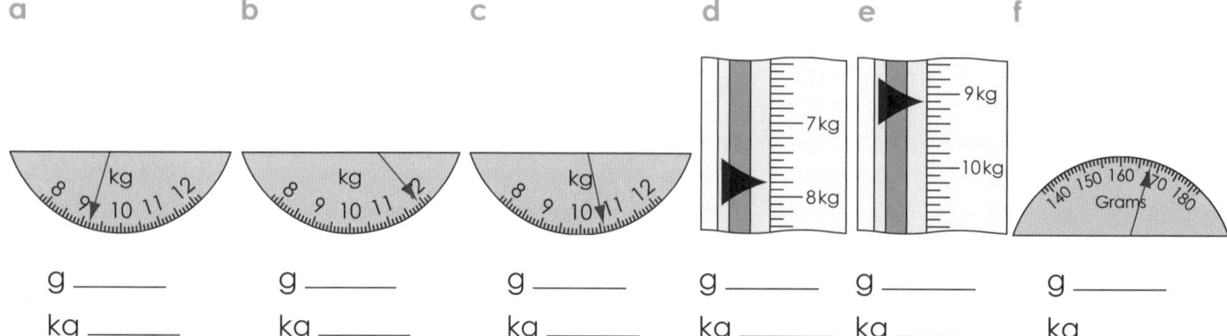

a g ______ kg ______
b g ______ kg ______
c g ______ kg ______
d g ______ kg ______
e g ______ kg ______
f g ______ kg ______

Complete the table to show the amount of water when the cylinder is filled to the marked levels.

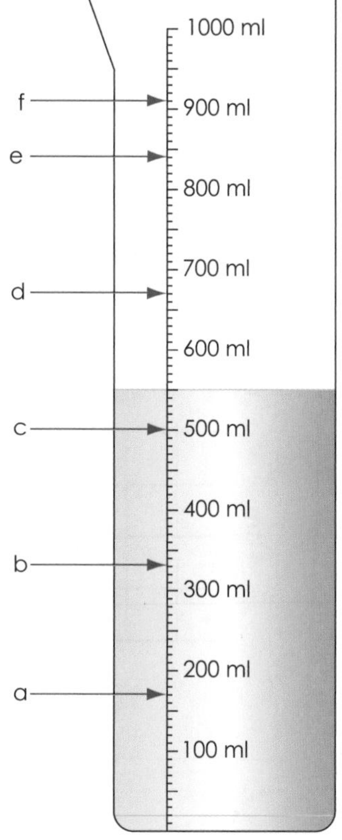

Level	millilitres	centilitres	litres
a	170 ml	70 cl	0·17 ℓ
b			
c			
d			
e			
f			

Go and do!

1 When visiting the vet's surgery a girl and her brother stood, in turn, on the weighing machine with their pet dog, Sandy.

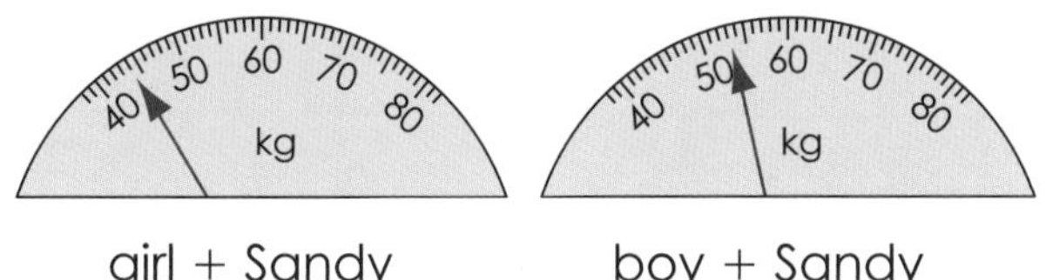

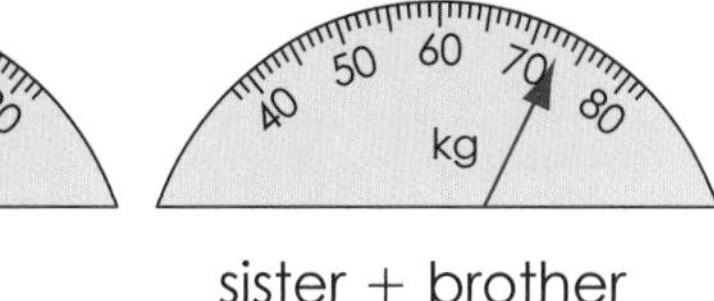

girl + Sandy   boy + Sandy   sister + brother

Find the weight in kilograms of:

a the girl ______ kg   b the boy ______ kg   c Sandy ______ kg

2 Go to the website: www.royalmint.com/corporate/facts/coins and find the information to complete this table.

Coin	Diameter	Weight	Thickness
£1			
10p			

a You make a column of £1 coins equal to your height. How much are you worth?

b 10p coins are placed edge to edge in a straight line. How much would your school raise for charity if the target distance is 0·1 km?

c Find out what you weighed at birth (1 lb ≈ 454 g). If the scales were balanced with £1 coins, what were you worth at birth?

Check up tasks

Ask your child: *How much longer is the line to f than to d? If the cylinder holds 650 ml of water, how many millilitres of water are needed to bring the level up to level e?*

Perimeter and area

The perimeter (P) is the distance all the way round a 2D shape and is measured in units of length.

Area (A) is the amount of surface space inside the perimeter and is measured in square units of length.

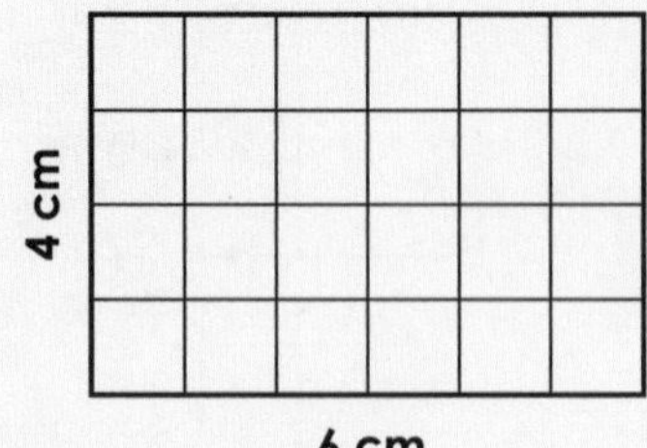

Formula

$P = 2 \times (l + b)$
$= 2 \times (6 + 4)$ cm
$= 2 \times 10$ cm
$= 20$ cm

$A = l \times b$
$= (6 \times 4)\ cm^2$
$= 24\ cm^2$

Top Tip for Parents

To avoid duplication of units in question 2, some children may find it helpful if they mark the starting point lightly in pencil.
Check that your child measures area in square units and reads these measurements correctly, e.g. 42 cm^2 as '42 square centimetres' and not as '42 centimetres squared'.

Exercises

1 Use the formula to work out the perimeter and area of these rectangles.

a
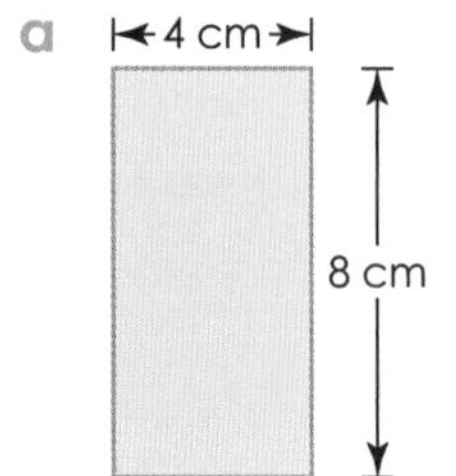

P = ______ cm
A = ______ cm^2

b 7 cm, 3 cm

P = ______ cm
A = ______ cm^2

c

P = ______ cm
A = ______ cm^2

d 6·5 cm, 5·5 cm

P = ______ cm
A = ______ cm^2

2 Work out the missing lengths and find the perimeter of each shape.

a
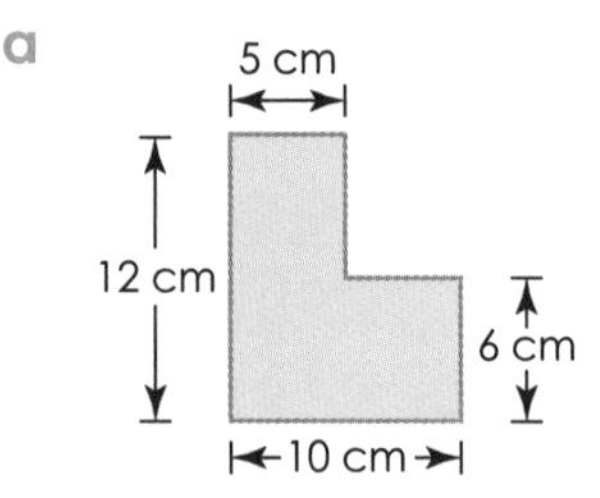

P = ______ cm

b
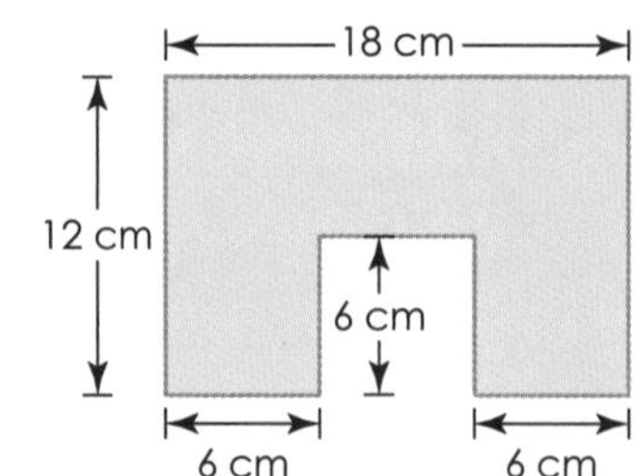

P = ______ cm

c
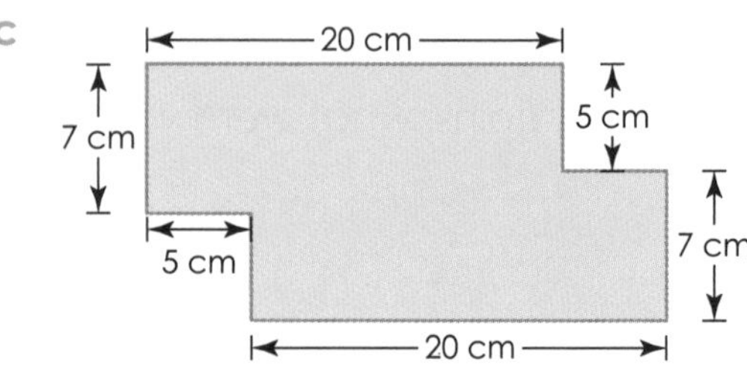

P = ______ cm

Here are three different ways to calculate that the area of this shape is 42 cm^2.

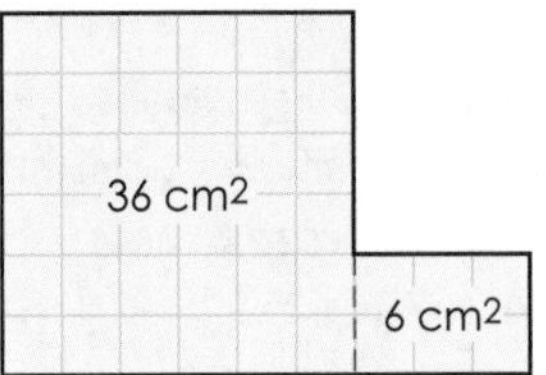

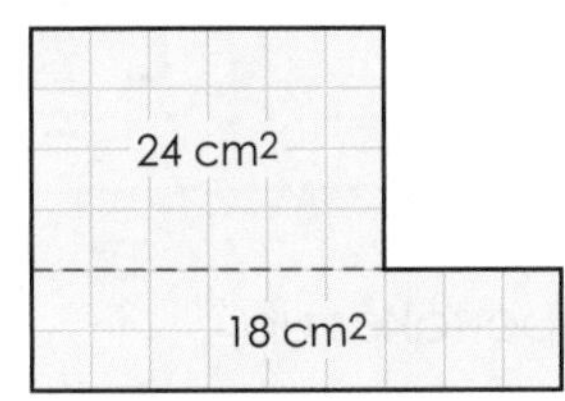

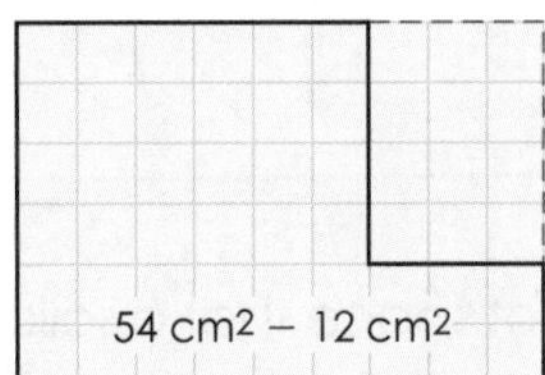

Choose a method to work out the area of each of the shapes in question 2.

These nets are drawn on 1 cm squared paper.
Work out the measurements and calculate the surface area of the net of each 3D shape.

a

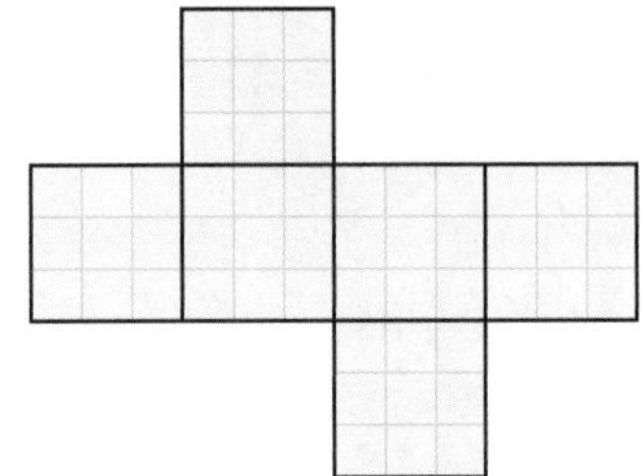

b

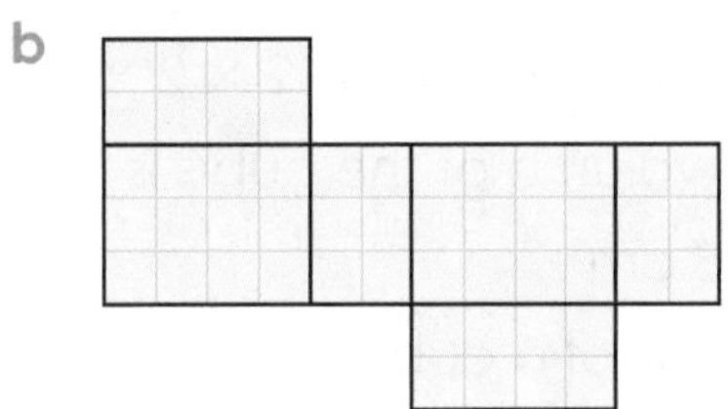

Go and do!

1 • Draw two rectangles, 6 cm × 2 cm and 5 cm × 3 cm, on 1 cm squared paper.
- Join the rectangles to make four different shapes. Find the perimeter of each shape.

2 In ancient Greece, mathematicians found the area of a triangle by transforming the shape into a rectangle.
- Copy each triangle on to 1 cm squared paper and cut it out.
- By making one cut, change each triangle into a rectangle and find its area.

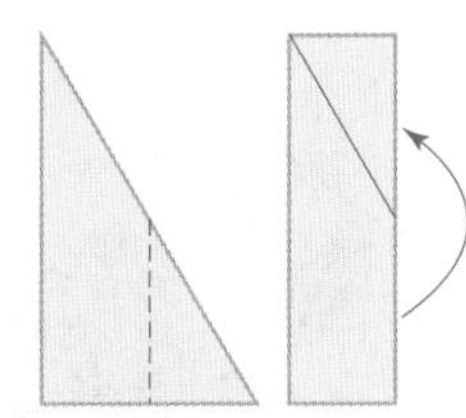

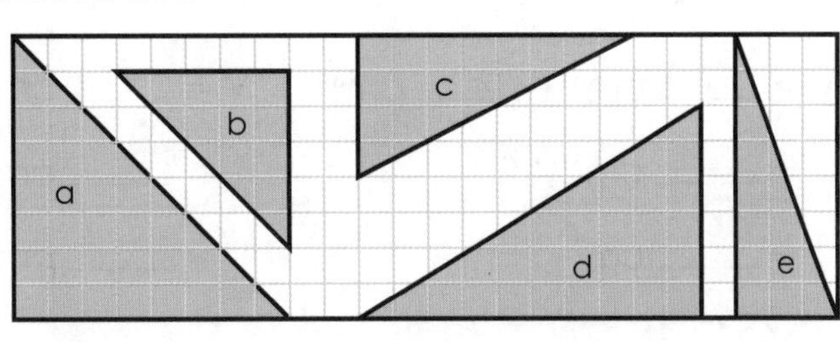

You need
- 1 cm squared paper
- Scissors

3 • Look out some cuboid boxes from your kitchen cupboard, e.g. cornflakes.
- Find a way to work out the surface area of each cuboid.

Check up tasks

Ask your child: *Which of the rectangles in question 3 has the greatest perimeter? Which method did you choose for question 3? How could you check your answer?*

Help! Keep Going! Good to go!

Volume

Volume is the amount of space that a solid shape takes up.

This cube is 1 cm long, 1 cm wide and 1 cm high.

It measures 1 cm × 1 cm × 1 cm so its volume is 1 cm^3.

We measure volume in cubic units.

In this cube each layer has 2 rows of cubes with 2 cubes in each row. So each layer has 2 × 2 = 4 cubes.

There are 2 layers so you need 2 × 2 × 2 = 8 cubes altogether. The volume of the cube is 8 cubic centimetres or 8 cm^3.

To find the volume of a cuboid we multiply its length by its breadth by its height. This gives us the formula: $V = l \times b \times h$.

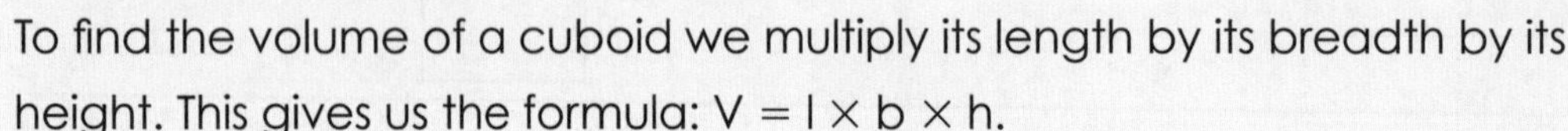

Exercises

1 Work out the volume of each cuboid by counting layers.

V = ______ cm^3

V = ______ cm^3 + ______ cm^3

= ______ cm^3 × 2

= ______ cm^3

V = ______ cm^3 + ______ cm^3 + ______ cm^3

= ______ cm^3 × 3

= ______ cm^3

2

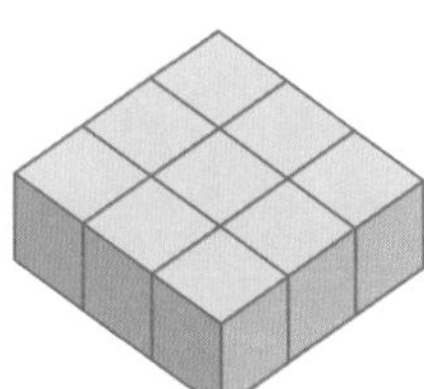

V = ______ cm^3

V = ______ cm^3 + ______ cm^3

= ______ cm^3 × 2

= ______ cm^3

V = ______ cm^3 + ______ cm^3 + ______ cm^3

= ______ cm^3 × 3

= ______ cm^3

Use the formula to find the volume of each cuboid.

a

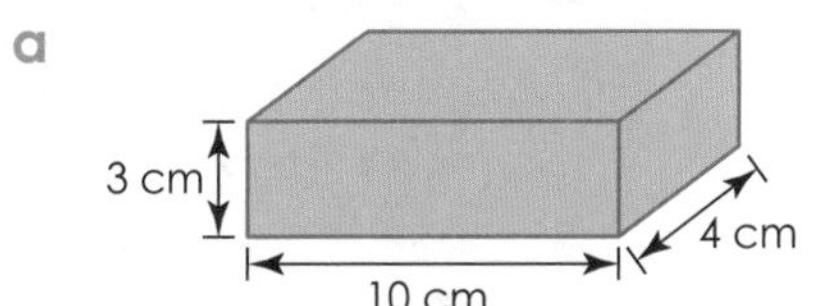

V = ______ cm³

b

4 cm
7 cm
9 cm

V = ______ cm³

c

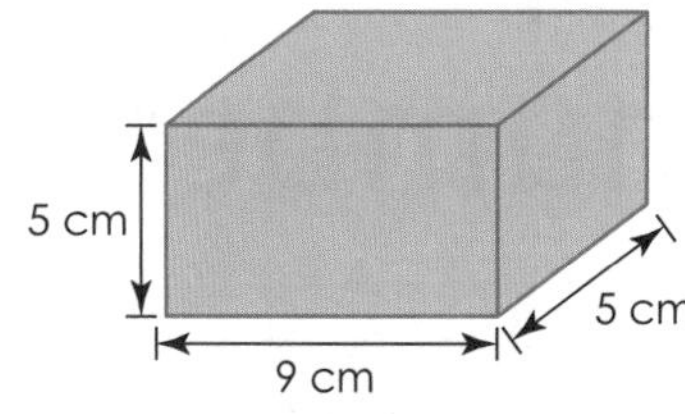

V = ______ cm³

Work out and write the missing dimension for each cuboid in the table.

Example

l = 5 cm
b = 2 cm
V = 40 cm^3
h = 40 ÷ (5 × 2) cm
= 4 cm

	a	b	c	d	e	f
length	5 cm		6 cm	3 cm		10 cm
breadth	3 cm	2 cm		3 cm	7 cm	
height		4 cm	1 cm		5 cm	5 cm
volume	30 cm^3	48 cm^3	72 cm^3	81 cm^3	140 cm^3	500 cm^3

Go and do!

- Find about six different cuboid shapes in your house, e.g. cereal packet, paperback book, pack of playing cards, carton for tube of toothpaste.
- Use a ruler to measure to the nearest centimetre the dimensions of each object and calculate its volume.

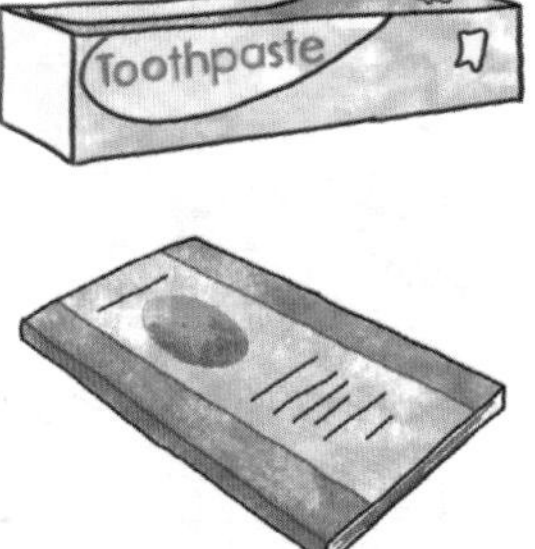

- Find a measuring jug and some plasticine or Blu-tack.
- Fill the measuring jug to the 200 ml mark with water.
- Make a lump of plasticine which you estimate will raise the water level by 50 ml and drop it into the water. Continue until you are as close to 250 ml as possible.
- Investigate what happens to the water level when you form the plasticine into these shapes: sphere, cube, cuboid and cylinder. What do you notice?

Check up tasks

Ask your child: *If a cuboid has a volume of 60 cm³, what might its dimensions be?*

Ask your child: *One of the edges of a cuboid is 9 cm. Its volume is 54 cm³. What might the other two edges measure?*

Square and triangular numbers

Top Tip for Parents

Encourage your child to look for a pattern and to use the pattern to find the next term in the sequences of square and triangular numbers and to answer the questions in Go and do!

In ancient Greece the Pythagoreans used pebbles or dots drawn in the sand to investigate which numbers could be shown as geometric shapes.

They made triangular numbers when they added together the counting or natural numbers.

$1 \quad 1 + 2 = 3 \quad 1 + 2 + 3 = 6 \quad 1 + 2 + 3 + 4 = 10$

They made square numbers when they added together the consecutive odd numbers.

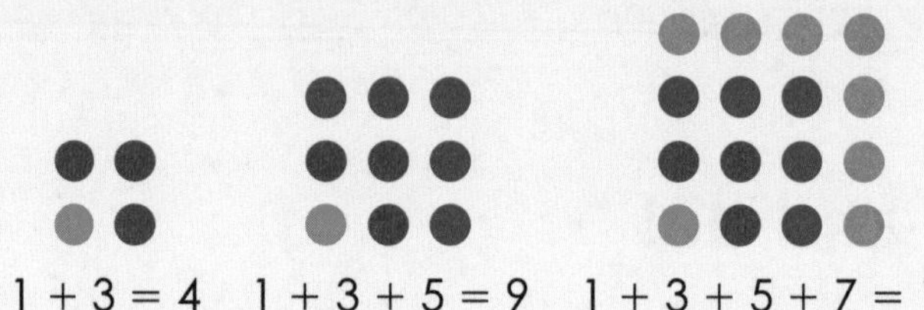

$1 \quad 1 + 3 = 4 \quad 1 + 3 + 5 = 9 \quad 1 + 3 + 5 + 7 = 16$

A square number is a number which has been multiplied by itself.
Four squared is written as 4^2. 4^2 means 4×4. $4^2 = 16$.

Exercises

1 Complete these tables.

a

Term	1st	2nd	3rd	4th	5th	6th	7th	8th	9th	10th
Counting number	1	2	3	4	5					
Square number	1	4	9							

b

Index notation	2^2		9^2		3^2		12^2		4^2	
Square number		49		64		25		121		36

2 Copy and complete each of the following.

a $5^2 + 5 =$ _____ b $7^2 + 7 =$ _____ c $12^2 + 6 =$ _____ d $9^2 + 21 =$ _____

e $8^2 - 12 =$ _____ f $10^2 - 41 =$ _____ g $6^2 - 28 =$ _____ h $11^2 - 19 =$ _____

i $3^2 + 5^2 =$ _____ j $9^2 + 4^2 =$ _____ k $8^2 - 7^2 =$ _____ l $10^2 - 6^2 =$ _____

Complete this table for triangular numbers.

Term	1st	2nd	3rd	4th	5th	6th	7th	8th	9th	10th
Triangular number	1	3	6	10	15					
Difference	–	2	3	4						

Go and do!

1 Find the difference between these square numbers.

a $2^2 - 1^2 = 3$ b $3^2 - 2^2 =$ ______ c $4^2 - 3^2 =$ ______

d $5^2 - 4^2 =$ ______ e $6^2 - 5^2 =$ ______ f $7^2 - 6^2 =$ ______

Look for a pattern and describe it. ____________________

Use the pattern to predict these differences.

g $20^2 - 19^2 =$ ______ h $45^2 - 44^2 =$ ______ i $99^2 - 98^2 =$ ______

2 This triangular pattern of numbers is named after Blaise Pascal (1623–1662).

a Look for a pattern and find the missing numbers.

b Total each row. Name the sequence of numbers.

____

c Circle the triangular numbers.

d Predict the total of the next row. ______ and check you are right by adding that row.

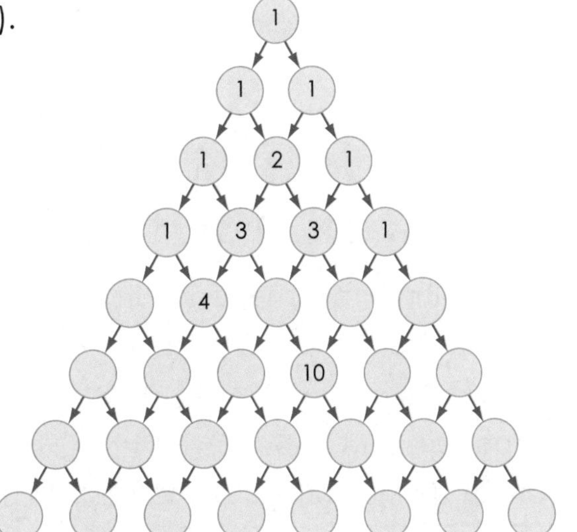

Total

______
______
______
______
______
______
______
______

Check up tasks

Ask your child: *Which two triangular numbers make the square number 64? Make 100? What is 82 + 12? Can you explain how you worked out the answer to* $20^2 - 19^2$*?*

Matchstick puzzles

We need to follow these steps to solve the matchstick puzzles.

Step 1 Make the diagrams for the first five matchstick patterns.
Step 2 Make a table.
Step 3 Look for a pattern.
Step 4 Write a formula for the number of matchsticks (M) and patterns (P).
Step 5 Test the formula by substitution.
Step 6 Use the formula to answer the question.

Top Tip for Parents

If your child is having difficulty in finding the formula for a pattern of matchsticks, then ask your child to say in words how the pattern is working and write down what your child says as a draft. The example on page 54 can be expressed as: The pattern is going up in threes so the number of matchsticks is found by multiplying by 3 and adding 1, or: The number of matchsticks is 3 times the pattern number plus 1. The next step is to translate your child's explanation into formal notation for algebra, e.g. $M = (P \times 3) + 1$ or $3P + 1$.

Example

If you continue this matchstick pattern, how many matchsticks will you need for the 20th pattern?

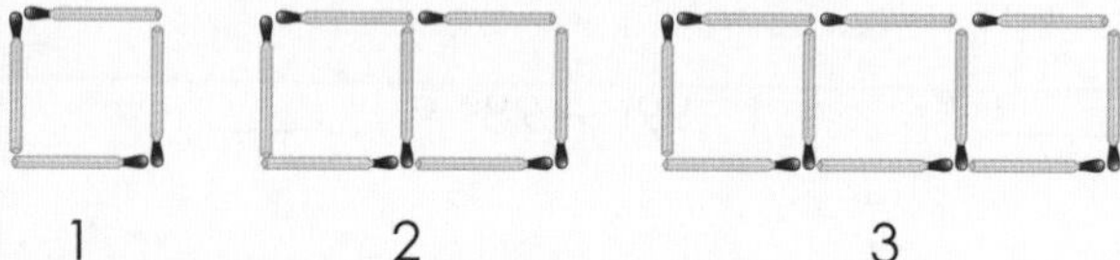

Step 1 The next two patterns in the sequence are:

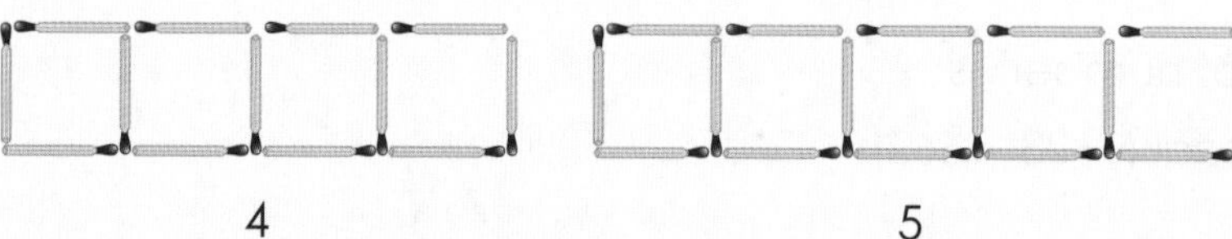

Step 2 Record the number of matchsticks for the first five patterns in the table.

Pattern number (P)	1	2	3	4	5	6	7
Number of matches (M)	4	7	10	13	16		

Step 3 We add three matches each time to make each new pattern. The 6th pattern is $16 + 3 = 19$. The 7th pattern is $19 + 3 = 22$.

Step 4 The formula is: $M = (P \times 3) + 1$ or $M = 3P + 1$.

Step 5 For pattern 5, $M = (5 \times 3) + 1 = 16$. For pattern 7, $M = (7 \times 3) + 1 = 22$.

Step 6 Pattern 20: the number of matchsticks is: $M = (20 \times 3) + 1 = 61$.

GO! Go and do!

You need
- A supply of matchsticks

1 For each matchstick pattern (a–d):
- Make the next two patterns in the sequence with matchsticks.
- Use the pattern to complete the table.
- Write a formula in terms of M and P that is true for every example.
- Test your formula by substitution for:
  - pattern 7
  - pattern 10
  - pattern 20

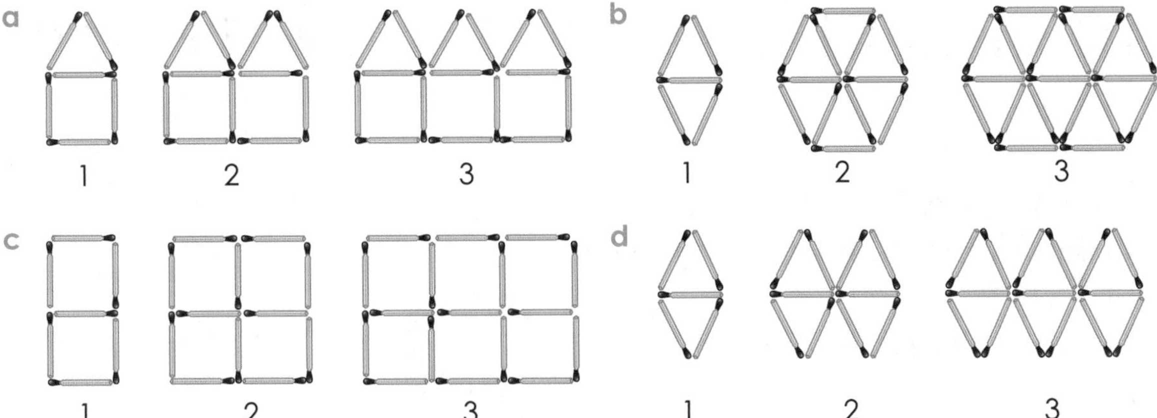

2 Find a way to make:

a 6 triangles using 12 matchsticks.

b 5 triangles using 9 matchsticks.

3 Large structures like cantilever bridges have to be as strong as possible. Engineers have found that the best shape for this is the triangle.

Using your matchsticks as struts, build the next two bridges in the pattern and complete the table. Find a formula and use it to predict the number of struts needed to build a cantilever bridge of pattern 25.

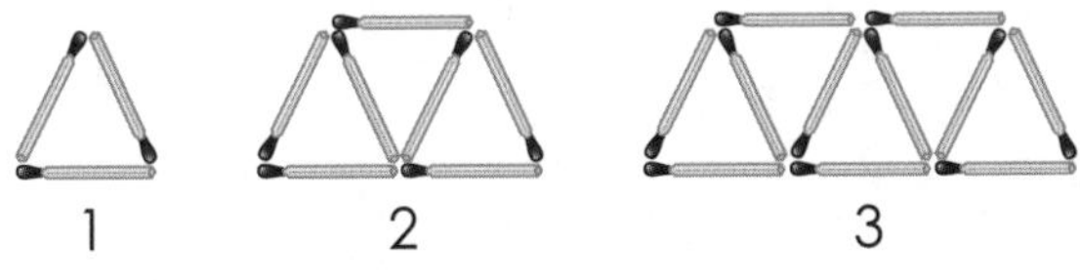

Pattern number (P)	1	2	3	4	5	6	7
Number of struts (S)	3						

Go and find!

Scotland's Forth Railway Bridge is the second longest cantilever bridge by span in the world. Search Wikipedia and find (a) where the world's longest cantilever bridge is located and (b) which country has the most cantilever bridges in the world's top 10.

Check up tasks

Ask your child: *How many matches were added each time in question 1b? Using the formula for question 1c, what is the 50th number in your pattern?*

Help! Keep Going! Good to go!

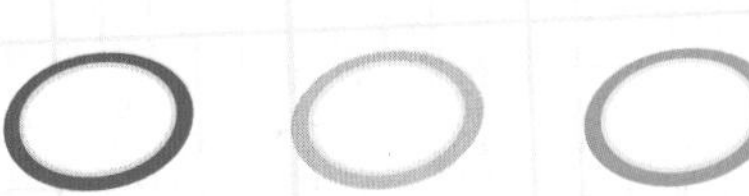

Letters for numbers

> **Top Tip for Parents**
>
> If your child finds the concept of using letters for numbers difficult, you may find it helpful to set some of the equations in a practical situation, as in the eggs example.
> When evaluating the expression 6e where e = 5, some children wrongly replace the e with 5 and write 65 instead of calculating 6 × 5 which gives the answer of 30.

In an equation, whatever is to the left-hand side of the equals sign (=) balances whatever is to the right-hand side.

Example

There are some eggs in the box and 4 eggs on the kitchen counter. There are 12 eggs altogether. How many eggs are in the box? $\square + 4 = 12$

If we take 4 from 12 that will equal the number of eggs in the box. $12 - 4 = 8$

We can also find the answer if we subtract 4 from each side of the equation. $\square + 4 - 4 = 12 - 4$ So $\square = 8$

In algebra we use letters to stand for unknown numbers. $n + 4 = 12$ so $n = 8$

If we add 4 to a number we write it as: $n + 4$ or $4 + n$

If we subtract 4 from a number we write it as: $n - 4$

If we multiply a number by 4 we write it as: $n \times 4$ or $4n$

If we divide a number by 4 we write it as: $n \div 4$ or $\frac{n}{4}$

Exercises

1 Work out the value of each Cuisenaire rod.

a = 1
b = 2
c = ☐
d = ☐
e = ☐
f = ☐
g = ☐
h = ☐

2 Use the value of the rods to complete these equations.

a $d + 6 =$ ______ b $h - 2 =$ ______ c $e + 12 =$ ______ d $g - 3 =$ ______

e $7c =$ ______ f $25d =$ ______ g ______ $b = 36$ h ______ $f = 54$

Now use the value of the rods to solve these equations.

a $6e + 4 =$ ____ b $20d - 11 =$ ____ c $8h + 14 =$ ____ d $12c - 12 =$ ____

e $4b + 3c =$ ____ + ____ $=$ ____

f $10h - 5e =$ ____ + ____ $=$ ____

g $5d \times 8a =$ ____ × ____ $=$ ____

Write an equation for the passengers on each bus and find the number that the letter stands for.

Example

$n - 7 = 18$
$n - 7 + 7 = 18 + 7$
$n = 25$

7 get off to leave 18

a

8 get on to make a total of 35.

____ k = □

b

26 get off to leave 14.

____ l = □

c

When 17 board the total is 39.

____ m = □

Go and do!

1 Make up some equations like those in question 3 where the answer is 60.

2 **On the cards** **An activity for 2 players**

- Take turns to choose 2 or 3 number cards and some sign cards.
- Place them on the table to form an equation in terms of x.

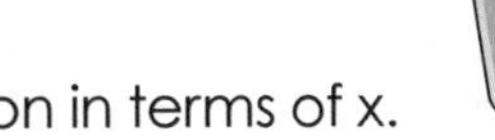

- Ask your partner to find the answer to your equation.

Check up tasks

Ask your child: *There are 500 pieces in a jigsaw puzzle. 80 pieces make up the frame. How many pieces make up the rest of the puzzle?*

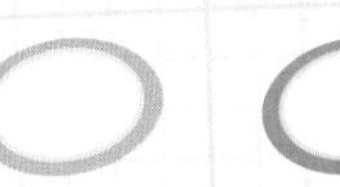

Help! Keep Going! Good to go!

Expressions and equations

> **Top Tip for Parents**
>
> Your child may mistake 2a for a × a. To counter this ask your child to refer to 2a as '2 lots of a', that is a + a.
>
> In question 2 you may need to remind your child of the order of operations where what is contained inside brackets is dealt with first.

We can use a letter as a symbol to represent an unknown number, e.g. in the equation $6 + a = 13$, the value of a is 7.

An expression is a way of writing word statements using symbols, for example:

A number add 11 is written as $n + 11$.

10 minus a number is written as $10 - n$.

4 times a number is $4 \times n$ or $n \times 4$ and is shortened to $4n$.

A number divided by 5 is written as $n \div 5$ or $\frac{n}{5}$.

A number multiplied by itself (or squared) is written as n^2.

A number multiplied by itself (or squared) and add 2 to it becomes $n^2 + 2$.

Add 2 to a number and multiply the answer by 3 becomes $3(n + 2)$.

In the expression $3(n + 2)$, n can take any value.

For example, if $n = 4$ then, by substituting n for 4 we get:

$3(n + 2) =$

$3(4 + 2) =$

3×6

$= 18$.

However, in the equation $3(n + 2) = 21$, we can work backwards to figure out that n must have the value of 5.

Exercises

1 Complete the table using the letter n to represent the unknown number.

Word statement	Expression
Add 5 to a number	
Subtract 6 from a number	
	$8 - n$
6 times a number	
	$8 \div n$
Multiply a number by 5 and then take away 2	
Divide a number by 4 and add 1	
Subtract 5 from a number and multiply the answer by 4	
	$8(n + 6)$

2 Substitute the values for a, b and c to find the weight of goods in each lorry when a = 10, b = 6 and c = 8.

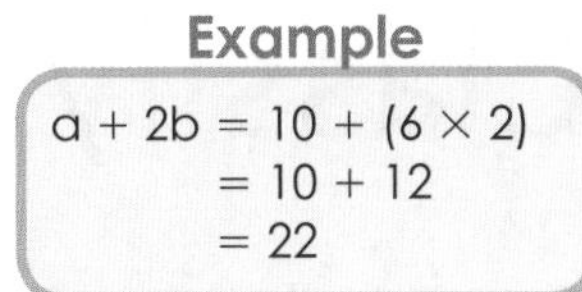
Example

$a + 2b = 10 + (6 \times 2)$
$= 10 + 12$
$= 22$

a

$2a + c =$
$=$
$=$

b

$7c - 9 =$
$=$
$=$

c

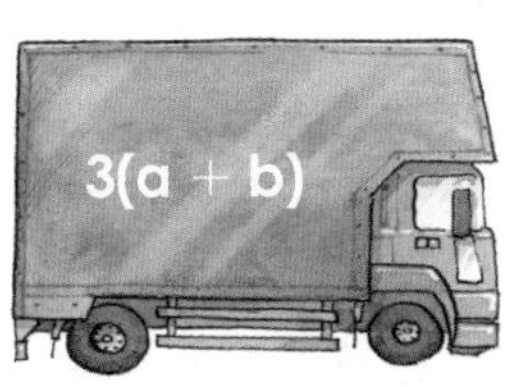

$3(a + b) =$
$=$
$=$

d

$5(c + 4) =$
$=$
$=$

3 The length of one of the fields (l) on Craigdhu Farm is double its breadth (b).
Find the perimeter of the field when:

a b = 80 m **b** b = 120 m **c** b = 200 m

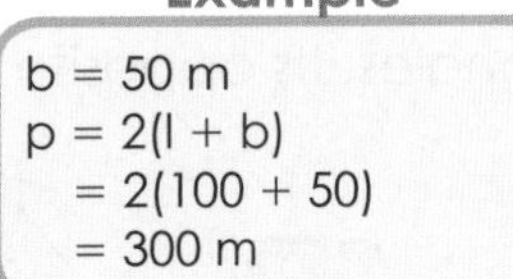
Example

b = 50 m
$p = 2(l + b)$
$= 2(100 + 50)$
= 300 m

Go and do!

1 In a magic square the magic number is the sum of each row, column or diagonal, e.g.
Row 1: $a - \not{b} + a + \not{b} - \not{c} + a + \not{c} = 3a$
The magic number is 3a.

a If 3a = 15, find the values for a, b and c.

b Investigate making magic squares where the magic number is 21. Use different values for a, b and c.

a – b	a + b – c	a + c
a + b + c	a	a – b – c
a – c	a – b + c	a + b

Go and find!

Station Taxis use a formula to calculate their hire charges.
Cost = (distance × 1·5) + 2
Find the cost of hiring Station Taxis to take you from your home to your nearest airport. To the centre of your nearest big city?

Check up tasks

Ask your child: *In the expression 3 + 5a, which operation do we perform first? If b equals 6, what is the value of the expression 30 – 4b?*

Classify 2D shapes

Quadrilateral facts

A **quadrilateral** is any 2D shape with 4 straight sides. Some quadrilaterals have unique features or **properties** and we give these quadrilaterals special names.

A **parallelogram** has its opposite sides equal and parallel.

A **rhombus** is a parallelogram with 4 equal sides.

A **kite** has 2 pairs of adjacent sides equal.

A **trapezium** has one pair of opposite parallel sides.

A **square** has 4 equal sides and 4 right angles. Its opposite sides are parallel.

A **rectangle** has 4 right angles. Its opposite sides are equal and parallel.

Top Tip for Parents

If your child is unsure whether or not he or she has replicated a quadrilateral, ask him or her to draw the two shapes on 1cm squared paper and to cut them out. If the two shapes can be fitted exactly one on top of the other, then the quadrilaterals have been duplicated.

parallelogram

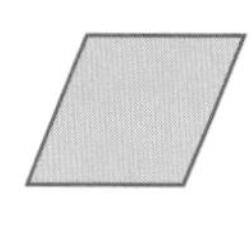
rhombus

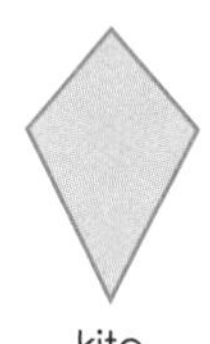
kite

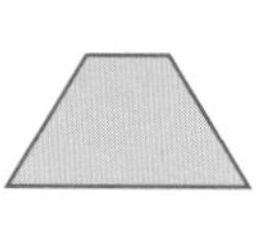
trapezium

square

rectangle

Go and do!

1 a Peter said: *'You can make exactly 16 different quadrilaterals on a 3 × 3 pinboard.'*
Is he correct? Investigate.
Remember, if you find shape 1, then shapes 2 and 3 are not allowed.

1 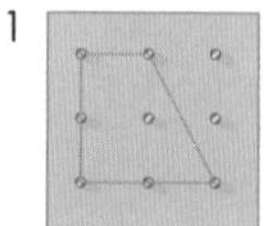

2 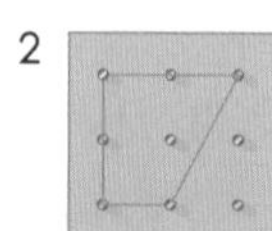

3 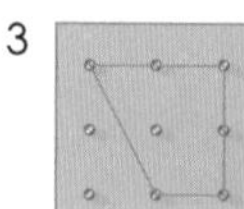

1 2 3 4

5 6 7 8

9 10 11 12

13 14 15 16

b Which quadrilaterals have at least 1 line of symmetry?
Which quadrilaterals have no pairs of parallel lines?
Which quadrilaterals have an interior angle greater than 180°?

2 Play these games with a partner. Use the quadrilaterals you drew for the pinboard investigation on the previous page.

a **Property pairs**

- Take turns to try to make a pair. On your turn say the number beside two of your quadrilaterals, e.g. 4 and 11.
- Your partner scores 1 point for making a pair by giving a property shared by both quadrilaterals.
- Your partner scores 1 bonus point by giving a different property which also makes a pair.
- The winner is the player with the most points after 10 turns each.

b **Name the shape**

- On your turn give your partner a maximum of three clues.
- Your partner must point to and name the quadrilateral correctly.
- Scoring:

Scoring:	Here are some clues you could use:
1 clue 3 points	*It has 2 obtuse angles and 4 equal sides.*
2 clues 2 points	*The shape has no line of symmetry.*
3 clues 1 point	*Opposite sides are equal, adjacent sides are not.*

- The winner is the first player to score 10 points.

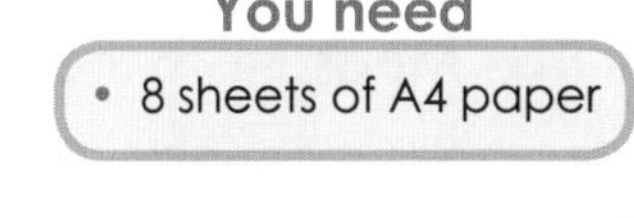

3 **Make a kite** Work with a partner

Follow the steps 1–6 to make 1 kite.

Make 8 kites.

Make a design using all 8 kites.

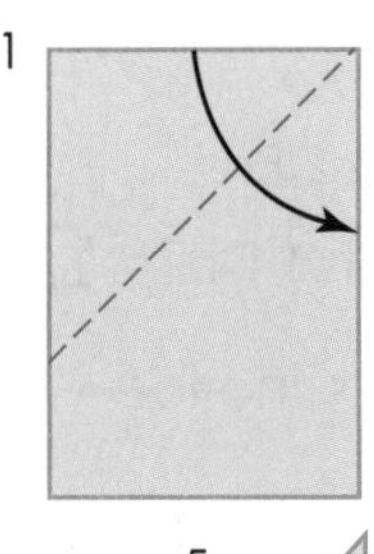

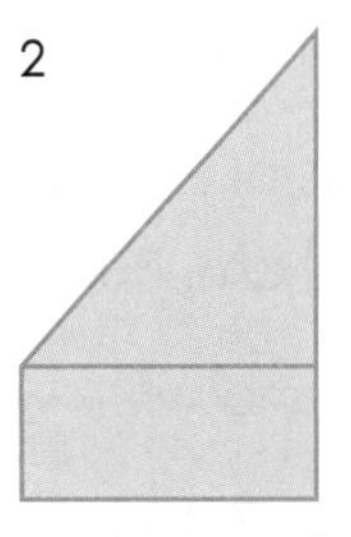

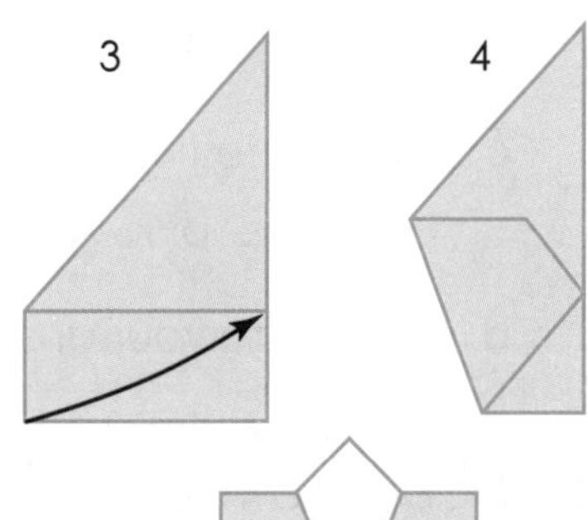

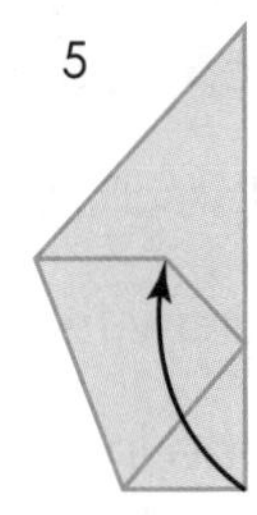

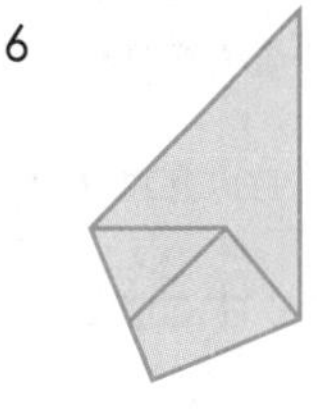

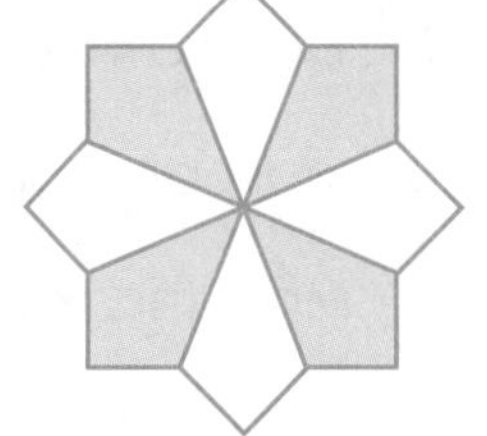

Check up tasks

Discuss with your child the answers to question 1b.

Draw 2D shapes accurately

Top Tip for Parents

Part of question 3b asks the child to calculate the area of the hexagon. If your child is 'stuck', you may want to direct him or her to the five shapes A to E which are cut from the square with sides of 8 cm in Go and Do! Question 2.

Important points to note

For each task it is important that you have a sharp pencil and a ruler.

When you measure the length of a line to the nearest millimetre, write your answer in centimetres, for example, write 54 mm as 5·4 cm.

The sign △ stands for triangle so △ ABC means triangle ABC.

Exercises

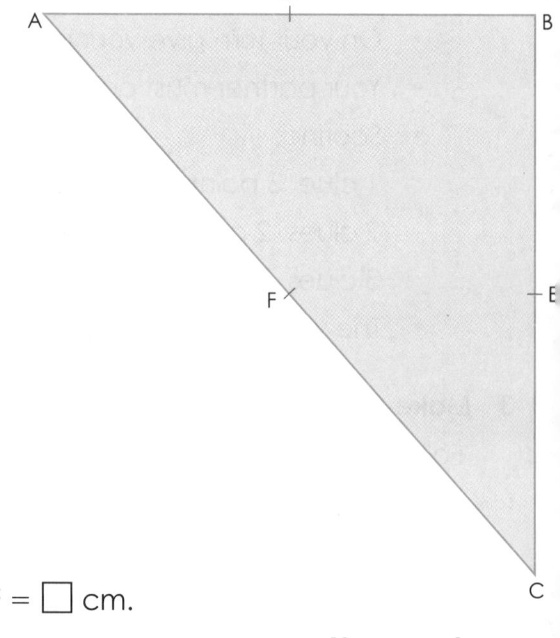

1 The midpoint of each side of △ ABC is marked with a dash and a letter.

a Use your ruler and pencil to join the midpoints DE, EF and FD.

b Measure to the nearest millimetre the lines:
AB = □ cm BC = □ cm CA = □ cm
FE = □ cm DF = □ cm ED = □ cm.

c Calculate the perimeters of △ ABC and △ DEF.
Perimeter of △ ABC = □ cm. Perimeter of △ DEF = □ cm.

d Compare your answers and write what you notice.

You need
- 1 cm squared paper

2 **a** Draw a 10 cm × 8 cm rectangle on to 1 cm squared paper.

b Mark and join the sets of midpoints as in the diagram.

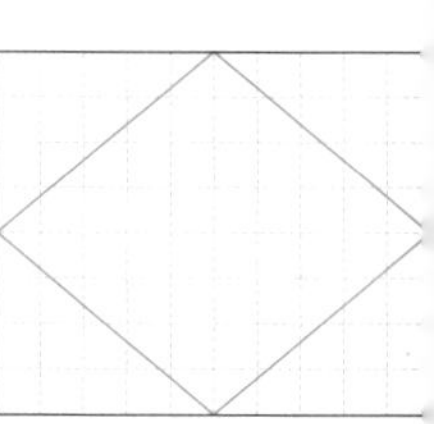

c Mark the midpoints of the rhombus and draw the rectangle.

d Repeat as above, with the midpoints of the inner rhombus.

e Measure and compare the lengths of pairs of parallel sides for:
- the outer and inner rectangles
- the outer and inner rhombuses.

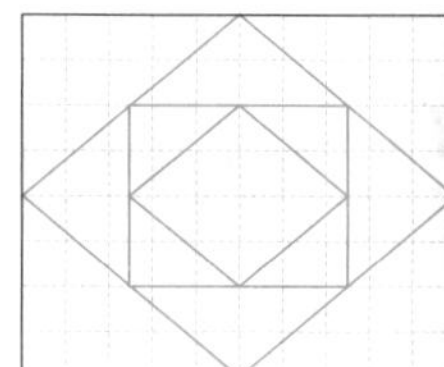

f Write about the relationship you notice.

Go and do!

You need
- Scissors
- Fine red pen
- 1 cm squared paper
- Ruler

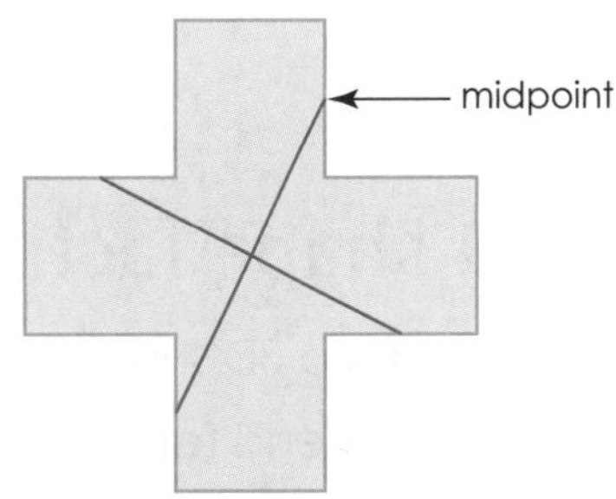

1 Use squared paper and a ruler to construct a cross with sides of 2 cm. Mark and join the mid points with a fine red pen or biro. Cut out the four pieces. Arrange the four pieces to make a square.

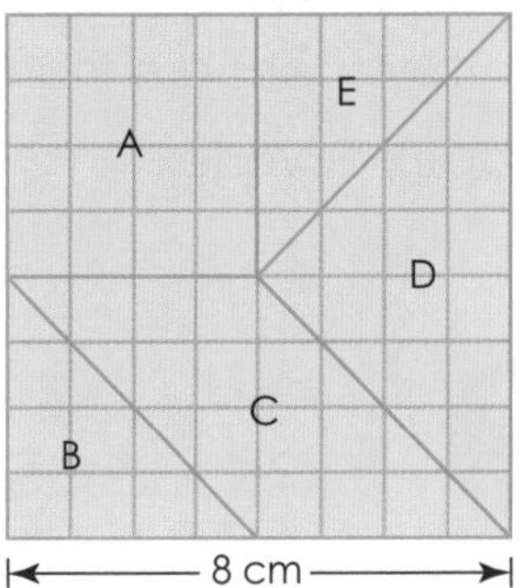

2 On 1 cm squared paper construct a square with sides of 8 cm. Rule the lines and label the shapes A to E. Carefully cut out the five shapes.

a Use shape E and two other shapes to make a square. Calculate the perimeter and area of the square.
Perimeter = ______ cm. Area = ______ cm^2.

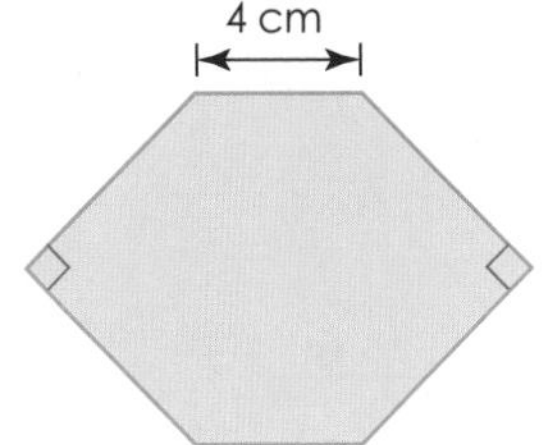

b Use all five shapes to make a hexagon. Calculate the perimeter and area of the hexagon.
Perimeter = ______ cm. Area = ______ cm^2.

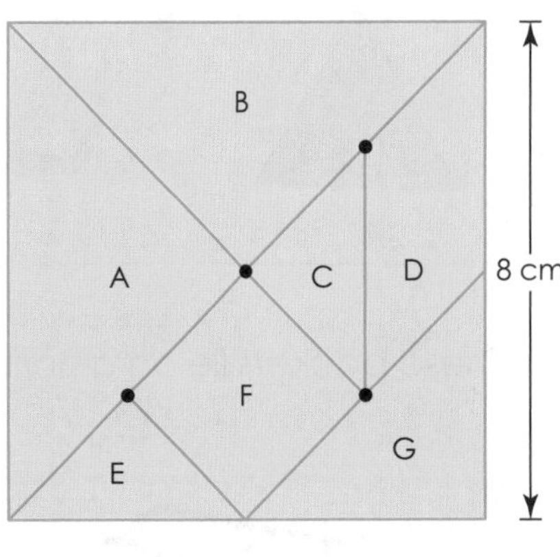

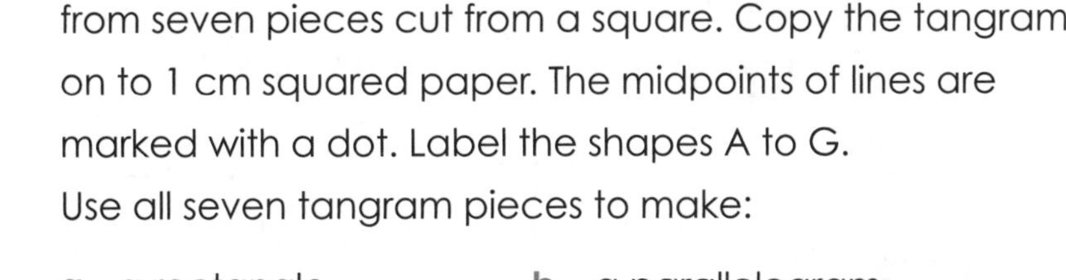

3 This Chinese puzzle called the tangram is made from seven pieces cut from a square. Copy the tangram on to 1 cm squared paper. The midpoints of lines are marked with a dot. Label the shapes A to G. Use all seven tangram pieces to make:

a a rectangle

b a parallelogram

Check up tasks

Ask your child: *What can you tell me about the lengths of the pairs of parallel lines in the triangle? The rectangle? The rhombus?*

Classify 3D solids

Top Tip for Parents

Some adults as well as children struggle to visualise 3D objects from 2D drawings. If your child has this problem with question 2, it would be helpful if you could display similar objects from your kitchen cupboard.

3D shape facts

A **prism** is a 3D shape with two parallel and congruent (or identical) end faces which are connected by rectangles. A **pyramid** is a 3D shape with a straight-sided flat base. All other faces are triangular and meet at a point called the apex or vertex.

Exercises

1 Name these solids.

a 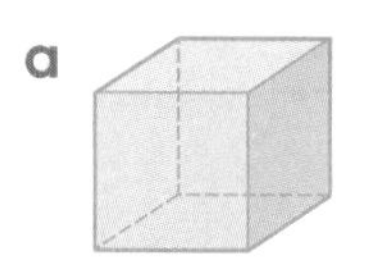 ______

b 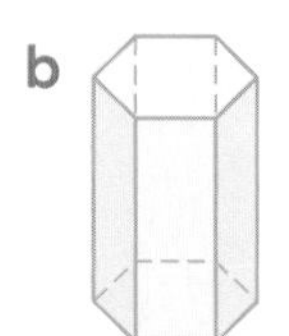 ______

c 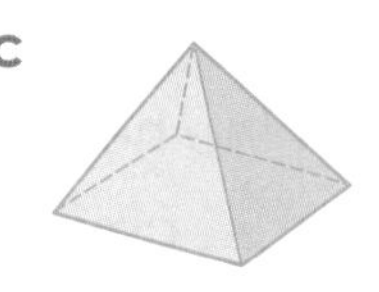 ______

d 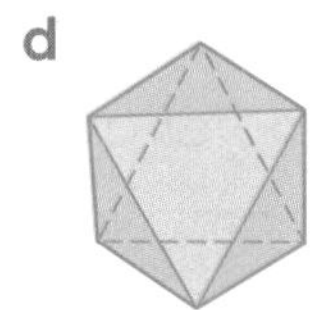 ______

e 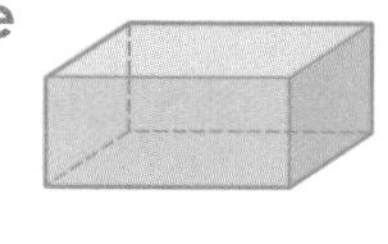 ______

f 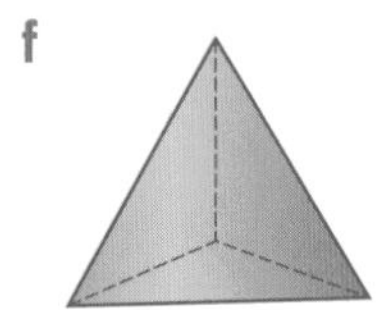 ______

g 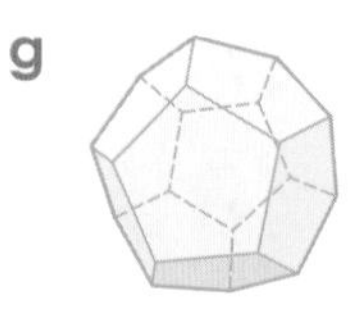 ______

h 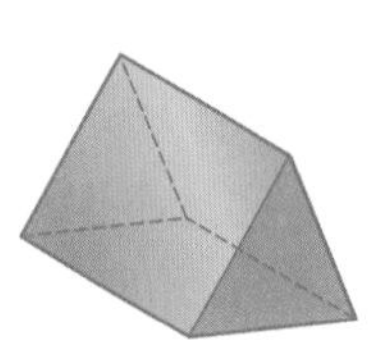 ______

i 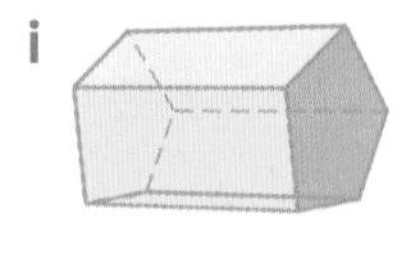 ______

j 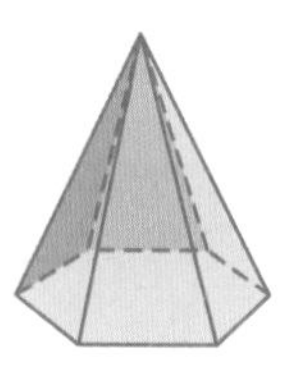 ______

2 These packets lie on a horizontal surface.

a Complete the table.

3D shape	Number of			
	Horizontal		Vertical	
	Faces	Edges	Faces	Edges
Pack of butter				
Block of cheese				
Packet of oatcakes				

b Write T(true) or F(false) for each statement.

// means parallel
⊥ means perpendicular

AB // DC ______ PS // QR ______ XY // ZY ______

DC ⊥ CB ______ SR ⊥ PQ ______ WX ⊥ WZ ______

Go and do!

You need

- A supply of A4 paper
- A thin sheet of cardboard about the size of A4 paper
- About six different sizes of tins from your kitchen cupboard to act as weights

1 **Paper pillars**

Investigate which shape of prism is the strongest by placing tins on the board until the pillars collapse. For each test make four identical prisms to support the board. What if … you made four cylinders?

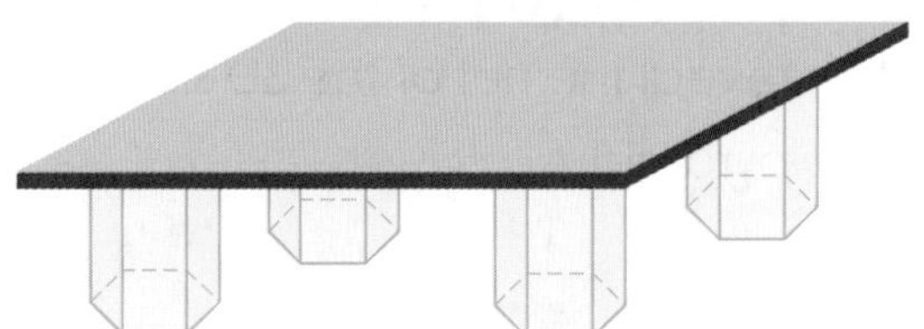

2 **Skeletal pyramids**

Martin said, *'If you make two square-based pyramids and join them together you can make an octahedron.'*
Is he correct? Investigate.

You need

- A supply of straws
- Plasticine or Blu-tack
- Scissors

3 **Investigating skeletal cubes**

a Look at the pattern of skeletal cubes and complete the table.

Skeletal cube	Number of cubes	Difference
3 × 3 × 3		–
4 × 4 × 4		
5 × 5 × 5		
6 × 6 × 6		

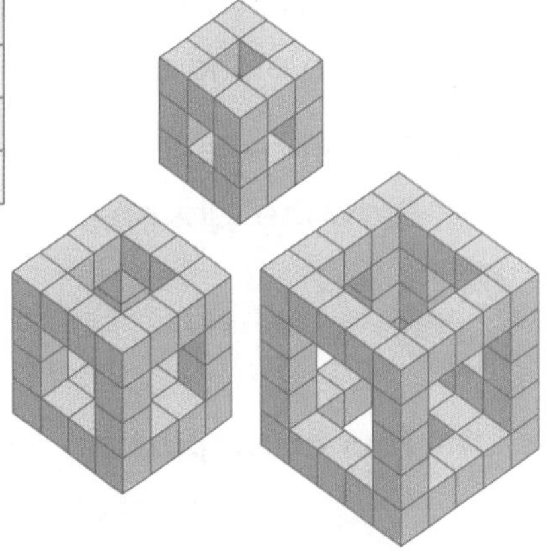

b Using the difference pattern, predict the number of cubes for a 6 × 6 × 6 skeletal cube.

Check up tasks

Say to your child: *Look at the pentagonal prism. Imagine I place one of its pentagonal faces on a table top. How many faces are vertical to the table? How many edges?*

Help! Keep Going! Good to go!

Nets of 3D objects

Top Tip for Parents

For the square-based pyramid the easiest net to construct is the one which has an equilateral triangle attached to each side of the square.

Net facts

A net is a flat shape which can be cut out and folded up to make a 3D shape.

This 3D shape is a square-based pyramid. Its base is a square and its four triangular faces are equilateral triangles. It has five vertices.

You can start at any vertex of the square-based pyramid and open it up to reveal the net of the 3D shape. Here are four different nets for a square-based pyramid.

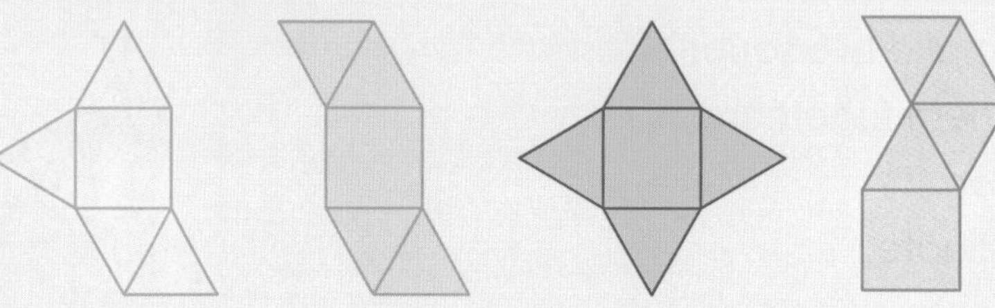

Exercises

1 a Suppose you want to construct the net of a square-based pyramid. Which of the above four nets would you select? Give a reason for your answer.

b To complete the net you need to put a tab on every alternate edge. Draw the tabs on the net of your choice.

Go and do!

1 **Four cubes puzzle**

- Draw four nets of this cube with sides of 2 cm on 1 cm squared paper.
- Draw a tab on every alternate edge.
- Colour each net as shown below.

You need

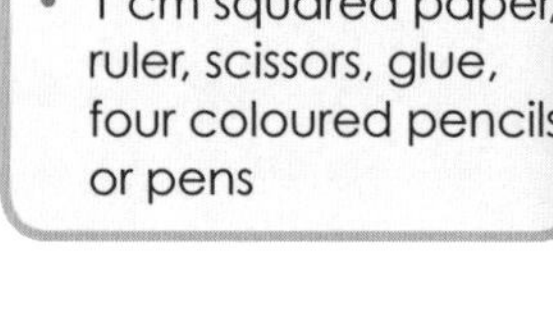

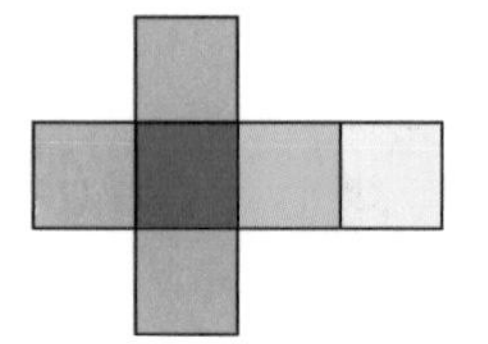

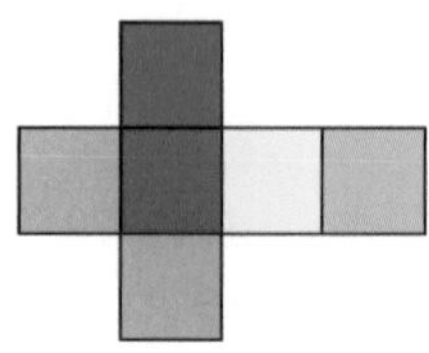

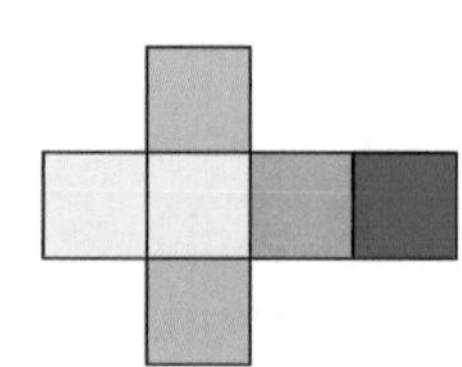

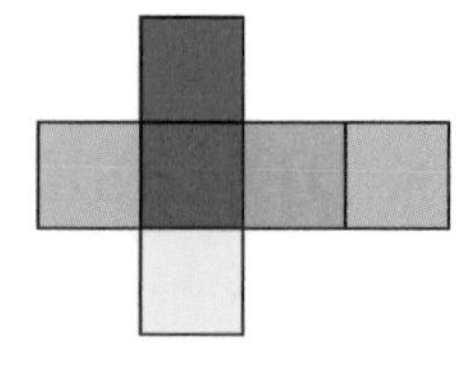

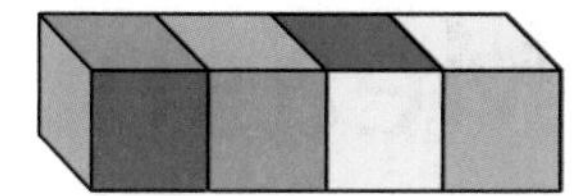

- Cut out, fold and glue each net to make your four cubes.
- Now make a rod of your four cubes so that all four colours are shown on each side of the rod.

2 Now construct the **net for the square-based pyramid** you chose in question 1.

- Draw a square with sides of 6 cm.
- Using your ruler and protractor, construct the four equilateral triangles with sides of 6 cm and angles of 60°.
- Draw the tabs.
- Carefully cut out your net.
- Score the fold lines and glue each tab in turn.

You need

- Ruler
- Protractor
- Scissors
- Glue

3 **Net for a triangular prism**

- Construct a rectangle with sides of 15 cm and 12 cm.
- Mark out three 5 cm × 12 cm rectangles.
- From the middle rectangle construct two equilateral triangles with sides of 5 cm.
- Draw the tabs.
- Carefully cut out your net.
- Score the fold lines and glue each tab in turn.

5 cm

12 cm

15 cm

4 **Three piece cube puzzle**

Work with a partner.

Using the net on the right, make three copies of the net of an oblique pyramid.

Then assemble the three oblique pyramids to make a cube.

For each net:

- score along the fold lines;
- fold up the net;
- glue the tabs in order.

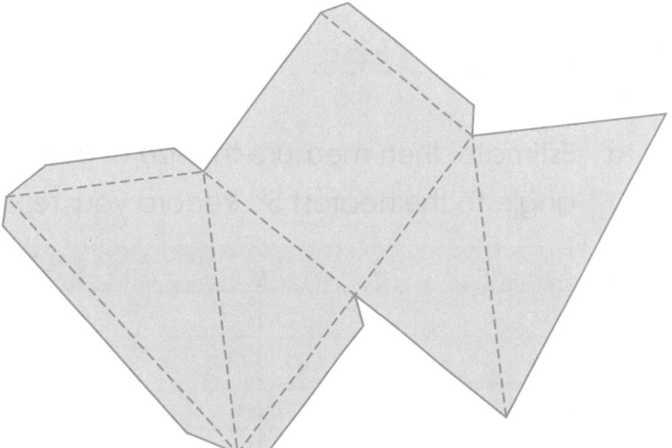

Check up tasks

Ask your child: *Which of the four nets for a square-based pyramid did you choose to construct for question 2? Can you give me a reason why you chose that one?*

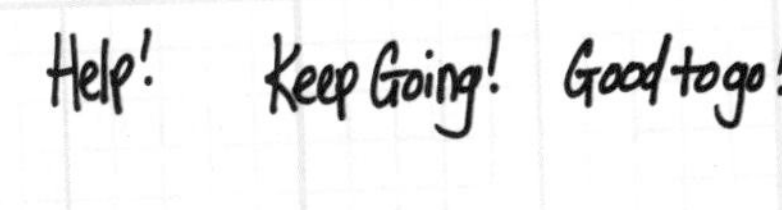

Measure and calculate angles

Top Tip for Parents

Encourage your child to estimate before measuring the size of an angle in terms of acute, obtuse or reflex.

Angle facts

An **acute** angle is between 0° and 90°.

A **right** angle is 90°.

An **obtuse** angle is between 90° and 180°.

A **reflex** angle is between 180° and 360°.

The sum of the angles on a straight line is 180°.
∠a + ∠b + ∠c = 180°.

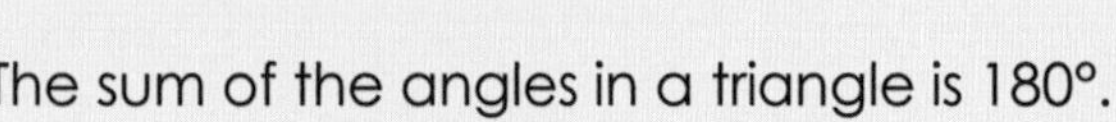

The sum of the angles in a triangle is 180°.

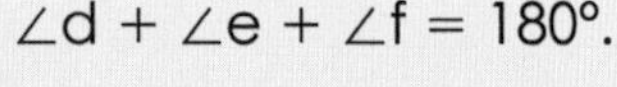

∠d + ∠e + ∠f = 180°.

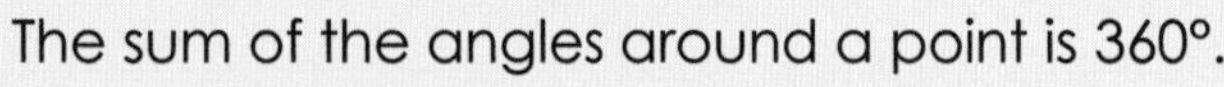

The sum of the angles around a point is 360°.
∠g + ∠h + ∠i + ∠j = 360°.

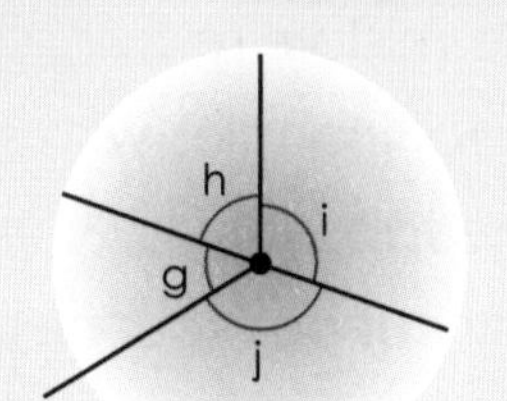

Exercises

1 a Estimate, then measure the size of each marked angle to the nearest 5°. Record your results in the table.

	Estimate	Measure
a		
b		
c		
d		
e		
f		
g		

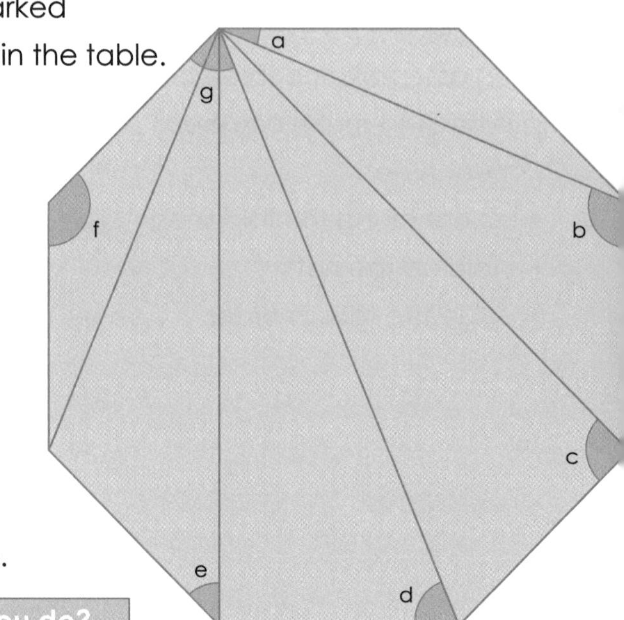

b Find the difference between your estimate and measure and work out your total score.

Scoring	Points	How well did you do?	
Within 5° of angle size	3	21 points	excellent
Within 10° of angle size	1	17–20 points	very good

a Measure and record the sizes of angles D, E and F.

∠D = ____° ∠E = ____° ∠F = ____°

b ABC is a straight line.

What should angles D, E and F total? ____°

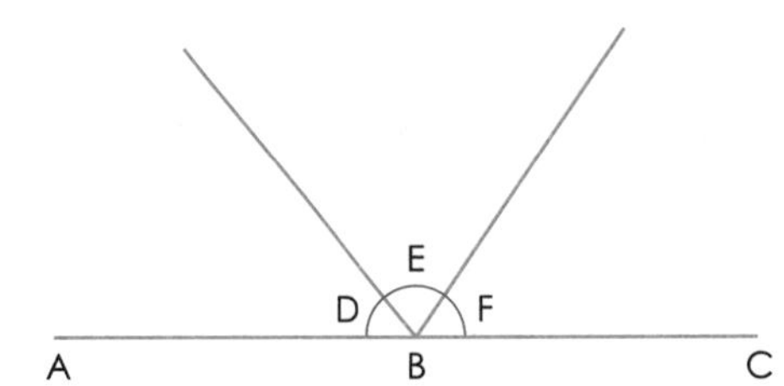

Work out the size of the missing angle in each triangle.

a

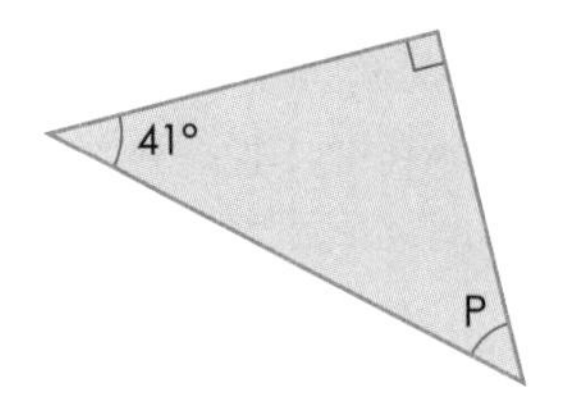

____° + ____° = ____°

180° − ____° = ____°

∠P = ____°

b

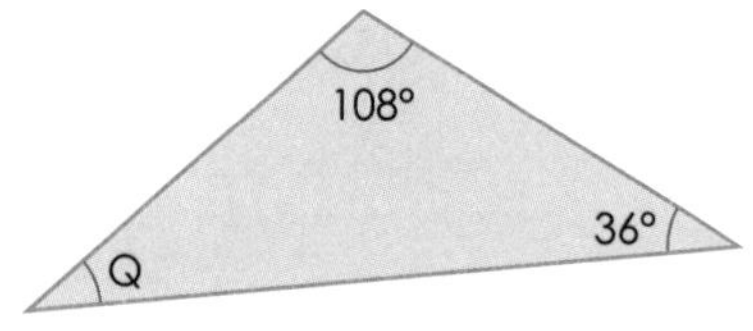

____° + ____° = ____°

180° − ____° = ____°

∠Q = ____°

Calculate the size of each shaded angle.

a

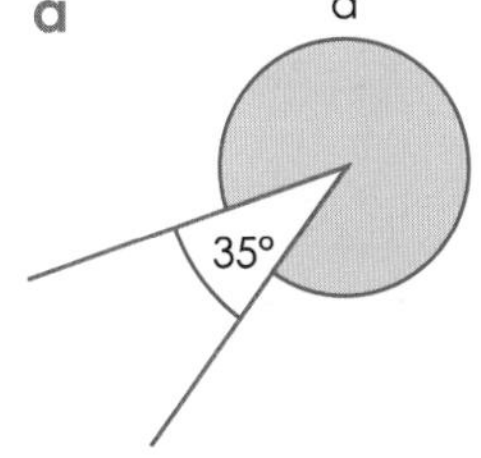

∠a = ____°

b

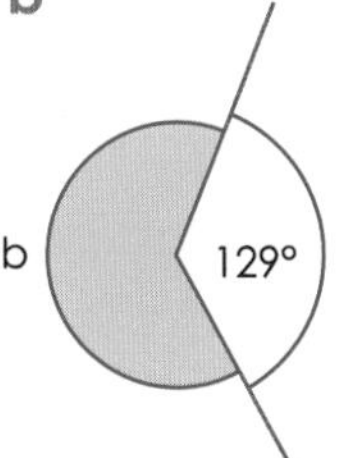

∠b = ____°

c

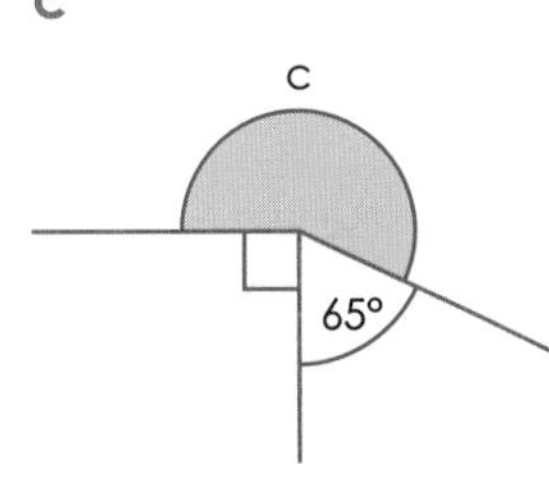

∠c = ____°

d

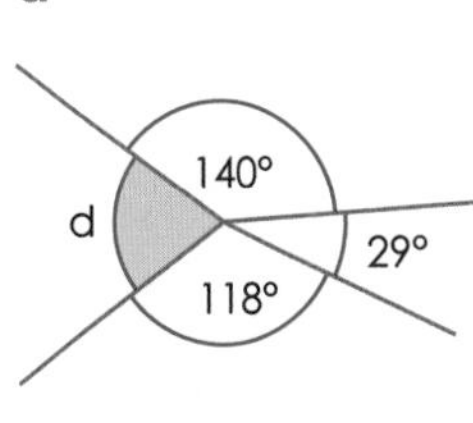

∠d = ____°

GO!

Go and do!

Angles in a clock face

1 Calculate these angles between the hands:

a the acute angle at 2:00 ____°

b the obtuse angle at 7:00 ____°

c the reflex angle at 10:00 ____°

d the acute angle at 5:30 ____°

e the obtuse angle at 9:30 ____°

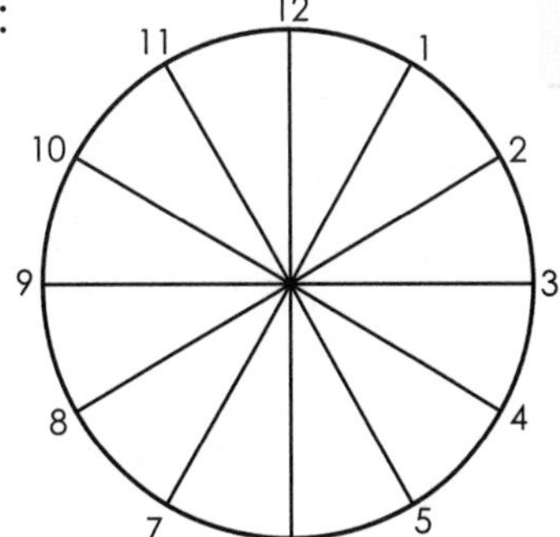

Note: The hour hand is halfway between the hours at the half hour.

Check up tasks

Ask your child: *In a triangle the base angles each measure 48°. How will you find the size of the missing angle? Can you tell me how you found the size of the shaded angle in question 4d?*

Help! Keep Going! Good to go!

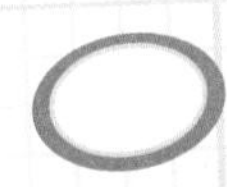

Drawing angles

You can construct any triangle if you know the length of two sides and the size of the angle between them.

Step 1

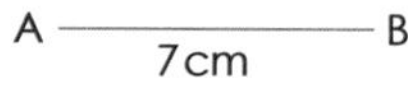

Rule a baseline AB 7 cm long. Place the crosswire of the protractor over A.

Step 2

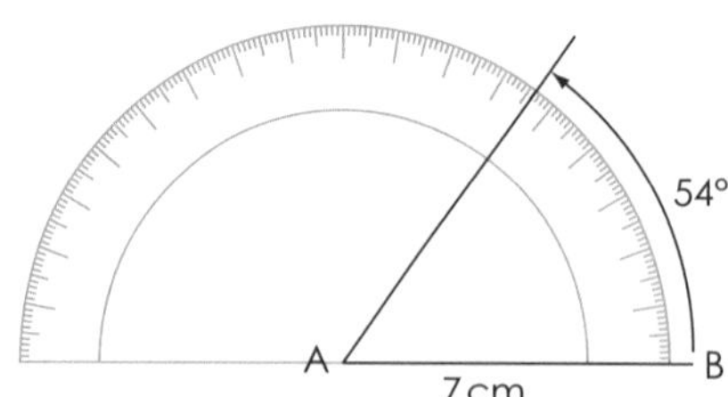

Count along the scale from 0°. Mark with a dot the position of 54°.

Step 3

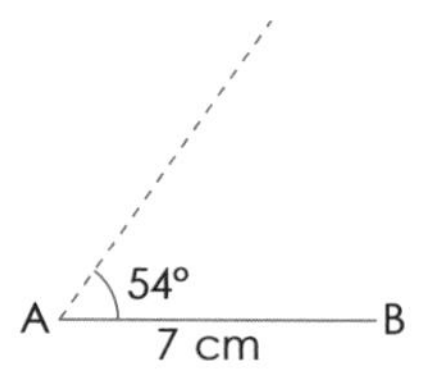

Join the dot to A with a lightly ruled line.

Step 4

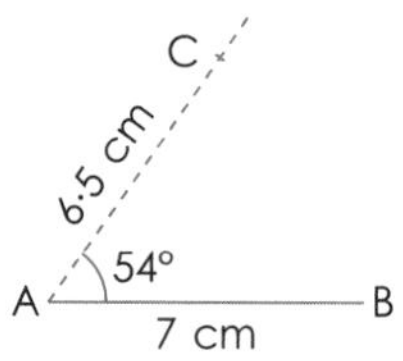

Measure and mark Point C, 6·5 cm from A.

Step 5

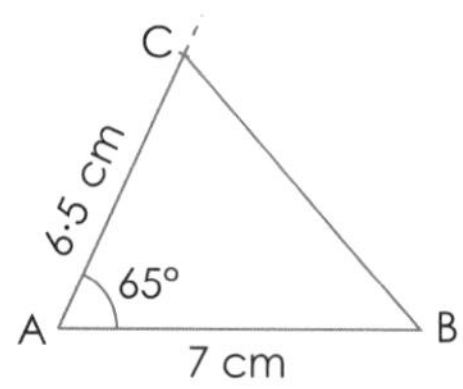

Rule lines to join C to A and C to B.

Top Tip for Parents

When measuring with a protractor, check that your child reads from the correct scale by counting round from 0° on the base line to the arm of the angle.

Exercises

You need

- Ruler
- Protractor

1 Make accurate drawings of these angles.

a

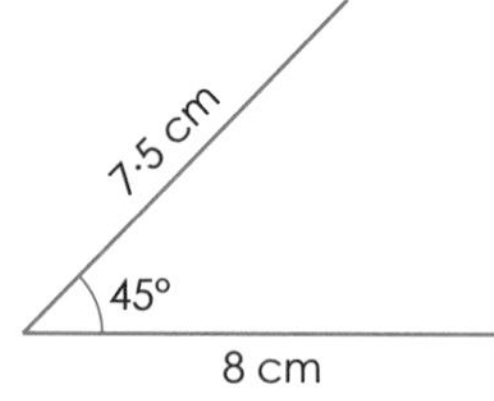

b

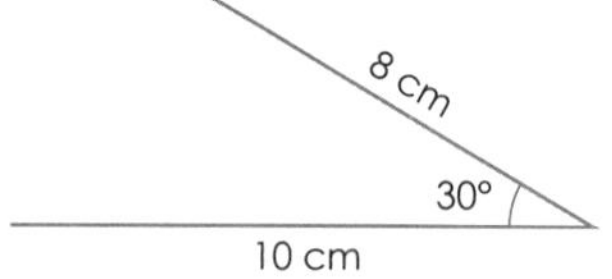

c

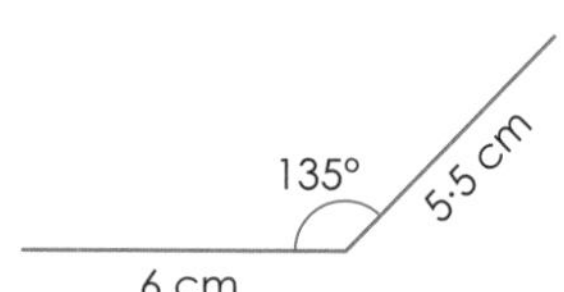

d

6 cm

100°

7·5 cm

e

8·5 cm

38°

6 cm

f

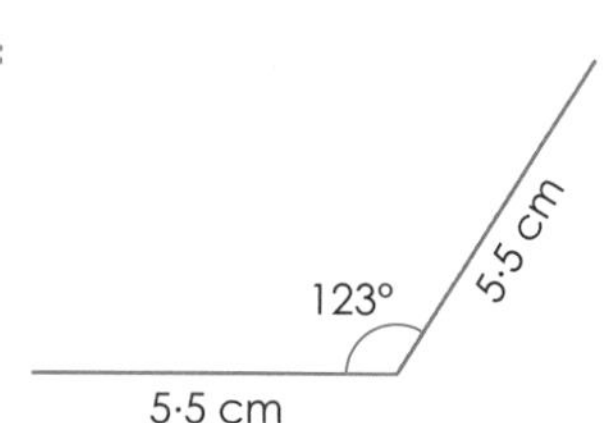

Use your ruler and protractor to construct these triangles.

a Draw a line AB 8 cm long. At A draw an angle of 80°. Extend the line AC to 8 cm. Label the point C. Rule a line to join C to B.

Angle B = _____°. Angle C = _____°.

b Draw a line KL 8 cm long. At K draw an angle of 65°. Extend the line KM to 5·5 cm. Label the point M. Rule a line to join M to L.

Angle L = _____°. Angle M _____°.

Now construct these triangles. Measure and label the lengths of the unmarked sides and the third angle.

a

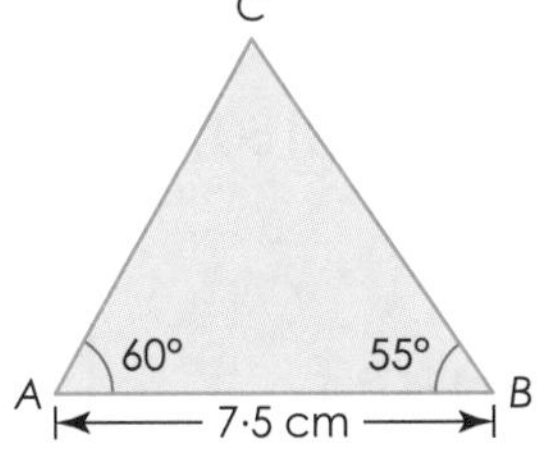

AC = _____ cm, BC = _____ cm, ∠C = _____°

b

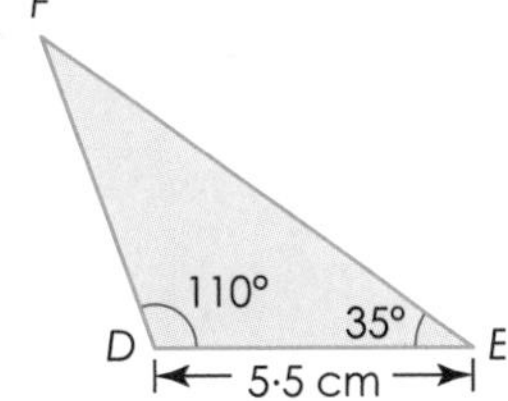

DF = _____ cm, EF = _____ cm, ∠F = _____°

These lines show the intersection of two roads. Copy the diagram accurately and calculate the other three angles. Write what you notice.

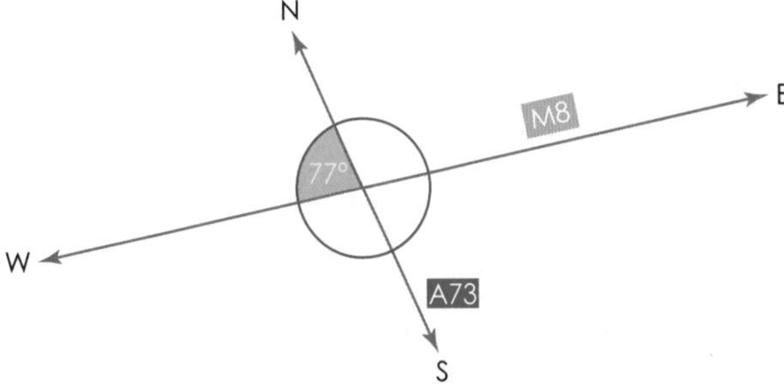

Go and do!

In Glasgow, the Clyde Arc crosses the River Clyde from Lancefield Quay to Govan Road.

- Locate the Clyde Arc in a road atlas. Investigate the sizes of the angles made by the bridge with the banks of the river.
- Which Scottish TV news programme features the Clyde Arc in the background to its broadcasts?
- Glaswegians have nicknamed the Clyde Arc the 'Squinty Bridge'. Why?

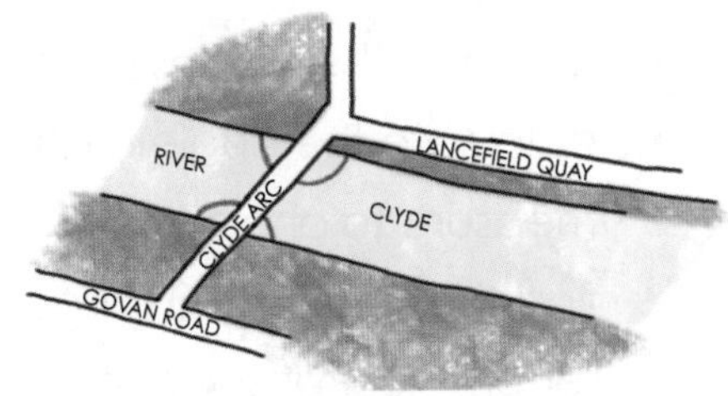

Check up tasks

Ask your child: *In question 2, how could you check that you have measured angles B and C correctly? What did you notice about the sizes of the angles in question 4?*

Help! Keep Going! Good to go!

Reasoning about lines and angles

Top Tip for Parents

If your child has difficulty in measuring the angles on these pages, say, 'You might find it helpful if you extend the length of the arms of the angle you are measuring.'

Angle facts

Thales (636–546 BC) founded the first Greek School of Mathematics at Miletus. By applying logical reasoning to the study of geometry he was able to prove that when two straight lines intersect, the vertically opposite angles are equal.

$\angle a = \angle b$ and $\angle c = \angle d$

$\angle a + \angle d = \angle b + \angle c = 180°$

Thales also discovered that the angles at the base of an isosceles triangle are always equal.

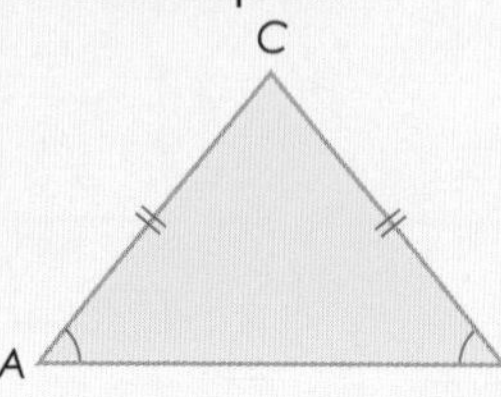

$\angle a = \angle b = 50°$

$\angle a + \angle b + \angle c = 180°$

Exercises

1 a Complete these statements about the sides in the parallelogram PQRS.

PS // ______ SR = ______

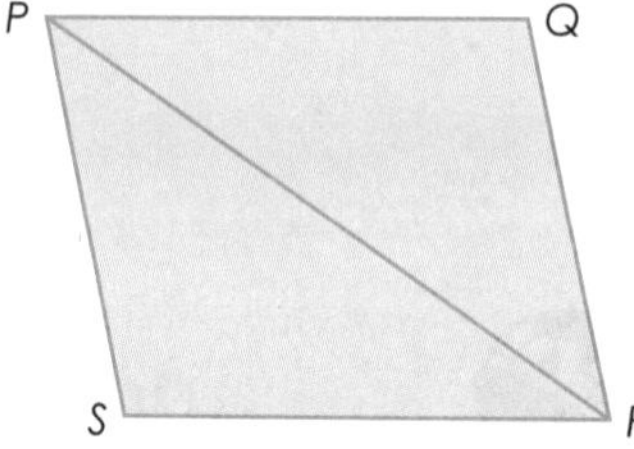

b PQ is an arm of ∠QPS. Name two more angles that have PQ as an arm.

∠ ____________ and ∠ ____________

2 For each diagram:

- measure the angles marked x and y;
- calculate the angle marked z;
- measure to check;
- find the angle total for each diagram;
- record your answers in the table.

a

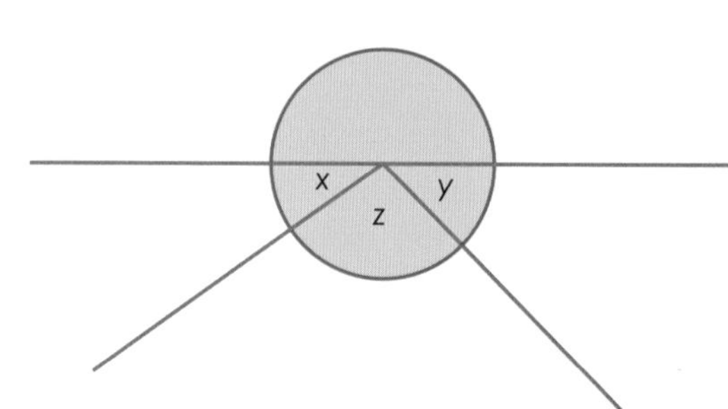

b

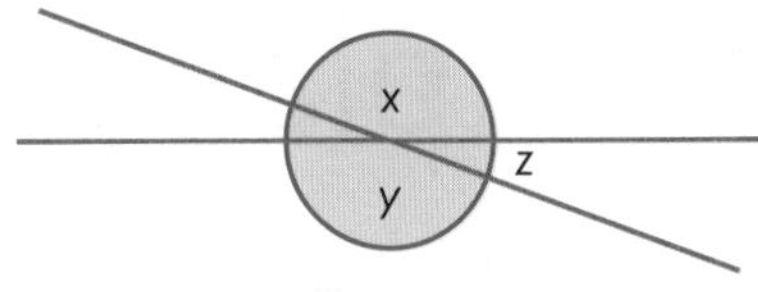

c

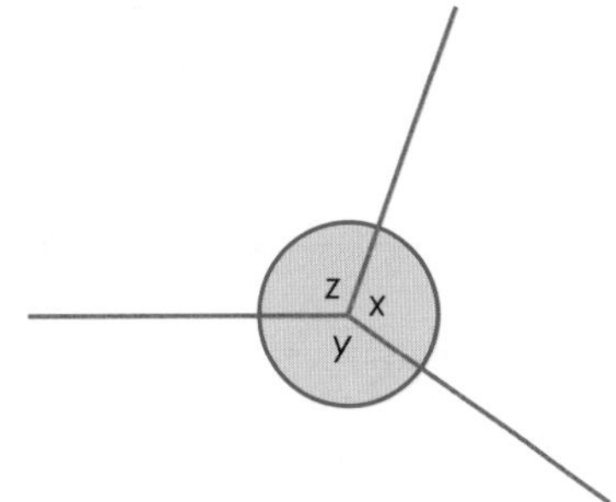

d

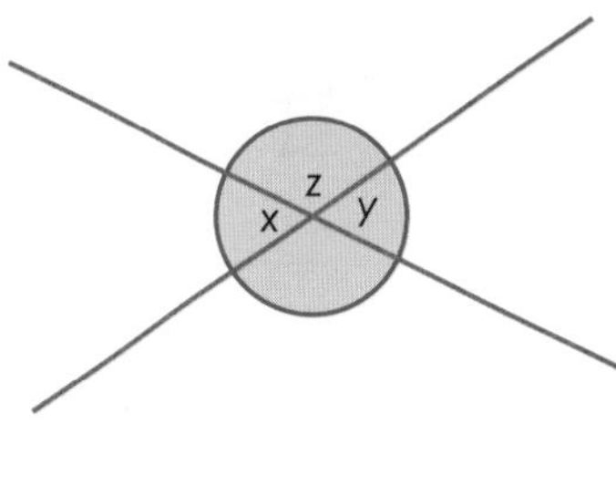

e

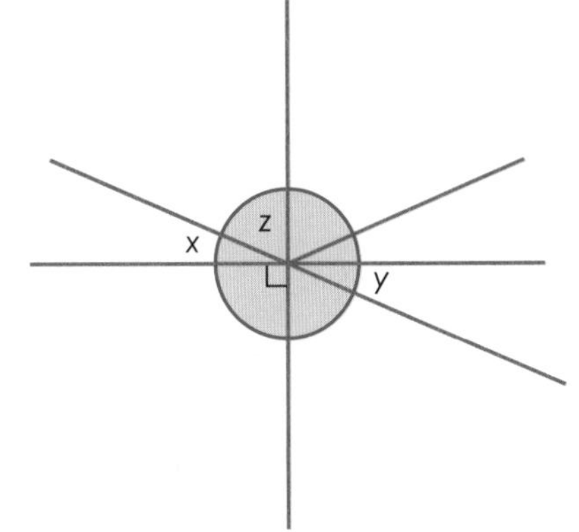

Diagram	∠x	∠y	∠z
a			
b			
c			
d			
e			

Go and do!

Angles in a regular pentagon

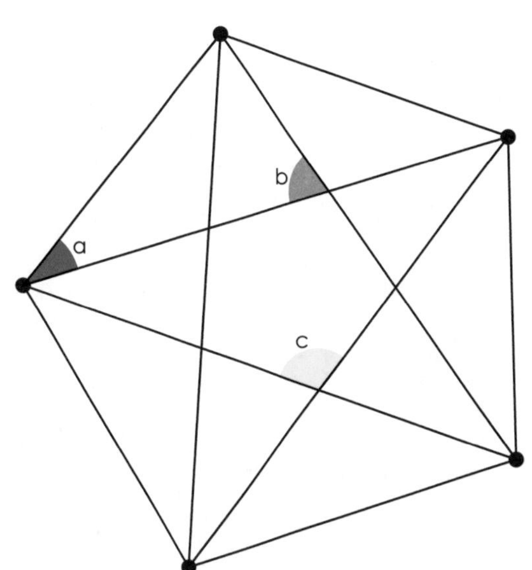

1 Measure the marked angles to the nearest degree.

∠a = ___°, ∠b = ___°, ∠c = ___°

2 Colour all the angles in the pentagon which are:

- the same size as ∠a – red
- the same size as ∠b – blue
- the same size as ∠c – yellow.

3 How many different isosceles triangles can you find in this regular pentagon?

Check up tasks

Ask your child: *Can you name three angles in Exercises question 1 that have P as a vertex? In question 2e, how did you find the size of angle z?*

Help! Keep Going! Good to go!

Compass points, maps and plans

Angle and degree facts

We know that an angle is a measurement of turn, that the amount of turn is measured in degrees and that when we make one whole turn, we turn through 360°.

Top Tip for Parents

When your child is drawing the floor plan using the scale 4 cm: 1 m, you may find it helpful to say that 1 cm on the plan will represent 25 cm on the floor.

8 point compass rose

We use a compass to find direction. In an 8 point compass rose we have 4 cardinal points, north (N), south (S), east (E) and west (W) and the intermediate points northeast (NE), southeast (SE), southwest (SW) and northwest (NW).

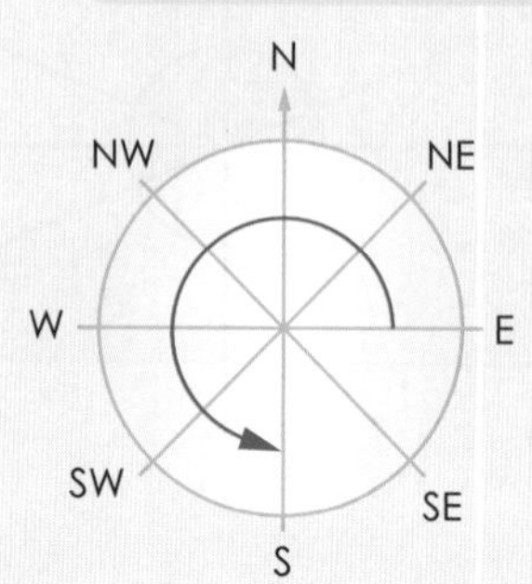

When you turn:

- clockwise from N to E you make a ¼ turn or 90°
- anticlockwise from E to S you make a ¾ turn or 270°
- clockwise from N to NE you make half of a ¼ turn or 45°.

Scale

When a map is drawn to scale all distances are carefully measured and made smaller in the same way, e.g. two villages, 5 miles apart, are shown on the map as 5 cm apart.

Exercises

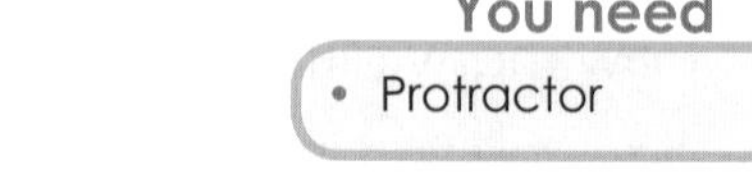

1 Work out the size of these angles on a compass rose.
Check with your protractor.

a

Size of angle = ☐

b

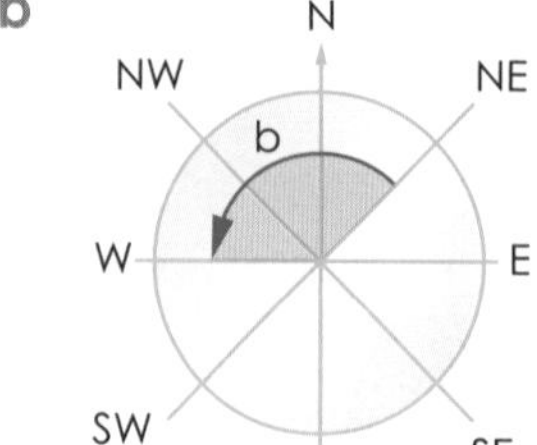

Size of angle = ☐

c

Size of angle = ☐

2 Write the direction you will face after turning through these angles:

a Face south. Turn clockwise through 135°. ☐

b Face west. Turn anticlockwise through 45°. ☐

c Face SE. Turn anticlockwise through 225°. ☐

d Face SW. Turn clockwise through 315°. ☐

You need
- Squared paper
- Measuring tape
- Ruler

Go and do!

Bedroom floor plan

- Choose a suitable scale, e.g. 4 cm: 1 m.
- Draw to scale the floor plan of your bedroom.
- Include the window and the door.
- Draw your furniture to scale.

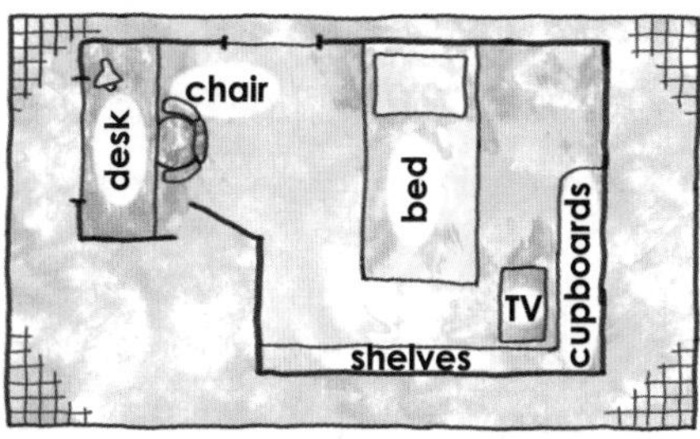

You need
- Map of Scotland showing scale
- Tracing of the compass rose
- Ruler

Go and find!

- Using the scale of the map and the compass rose tracing, calculate the distance and direction of travel from Stirling to five places on the map.
- Repeat, as above, for five more cities or towns. Include the place nearest to where you live.
- Now find a Road Atlas which has a Distance Chart. Compare your answers with those given by the Road Atlas Distance Chart. What do you notice? Can you explain why this is so?
- What does the phrase '*as the crow flies*' mean when talking about the distance between two places? How might a helicopter pilot measure the distance between two places? What about a taxi driver?

Check up tasks

Ask your child: *What is the amount of a clockwise turn from S to NE? From SE to SW? What if each turn was anticlockwise?*

Ask your child: *In your floor plan, how wide is your bedroom window? How long is your bed?*

Co-ordinates

Did you know?

The Frenchman, René Descartes (1596–1650) gave his name to Cartesian co-ordinates which are used to plot positions on a grid.

The lines in the grid are numbered for both horizontal and vertical axes from the origin (0, 0). The point at which two lines intersect is shown by a pair of numbers called co-ordinates. By convention, the movement is along (the corridor) then up (the stairs) so the horizontal co-ordinate comes before the vertical one. The point (3, 5) is marked and labelled.

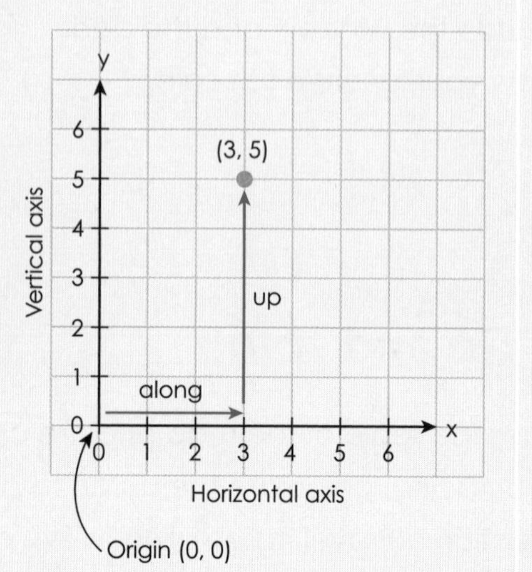

Top Tip for Parents

When writing the co-ordinates of a point, the phrase: 'along the corridor then up the stairs' will help your child to remember to give the x-co-ordinate first.

Exercises

1 At the school fair people have to guess where the treasure is buried.

a Complete this list of guesses.

A (0, __)
B (3, __)
C (__, 3)
D (__, 3)
E (2, __)
F (__, __)
G (__, __)
H (__, __)

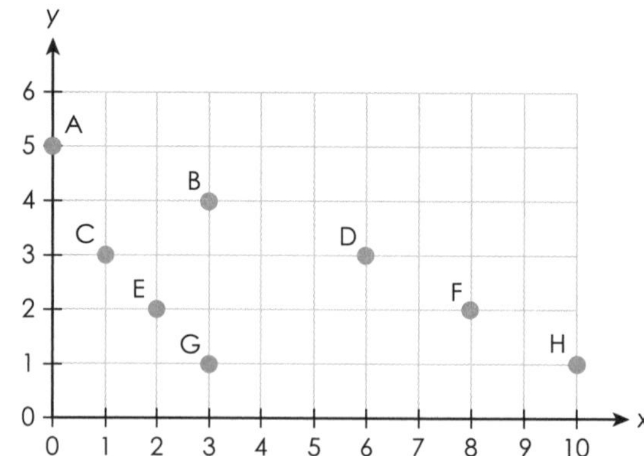

b Two unclaimed prizes are buried at P (7, 6) and Q (9, 0). Plot these points on the co-ordinate grid.

a Three of the vertices of a rectangle are plotted on each grid. Find the 4th vertex.

b Write the co-ordinates of the 4th vertex of each rectangle.

Grid A (☐, ☐)

Grid B (☐, ☐).

Grid A

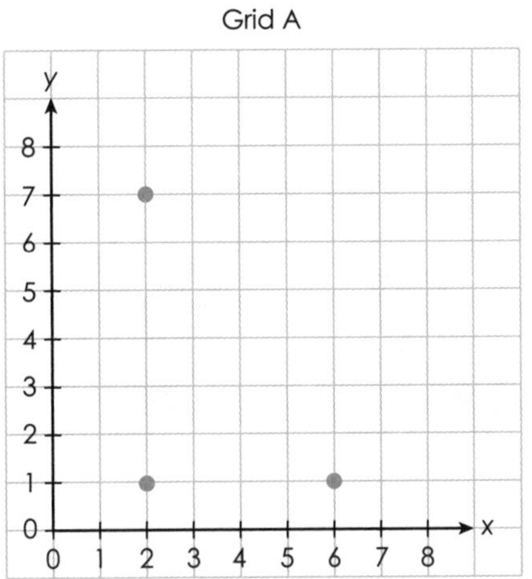

Grid B

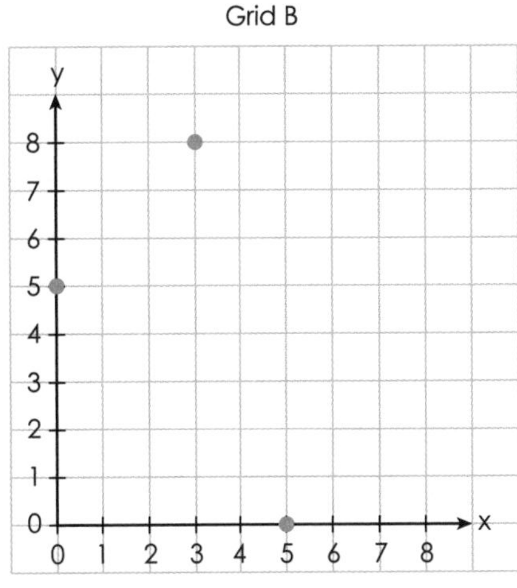

Go and do!

Work with a partner.

You need

- 1 red pen, 1 blue pen
- A 1–6 dice. Blank out the 6 and write 0.

1 **3 co-ordinates in a row**

- Take turns to roll the dice twice. The first roll gives the x-axis, the second roll gives the y-axis.
- Colour the co-ordinates of the point shown by two rolls of the dice.
- If the co-ordinates are already coloured in:
  – by your opponent's colour, you miss a turn
  – by one of your own colours, roll the dice again.
- The winner is the first player to have three coloured co-ordinates in a row, either horizontally, vertically or diagonally.

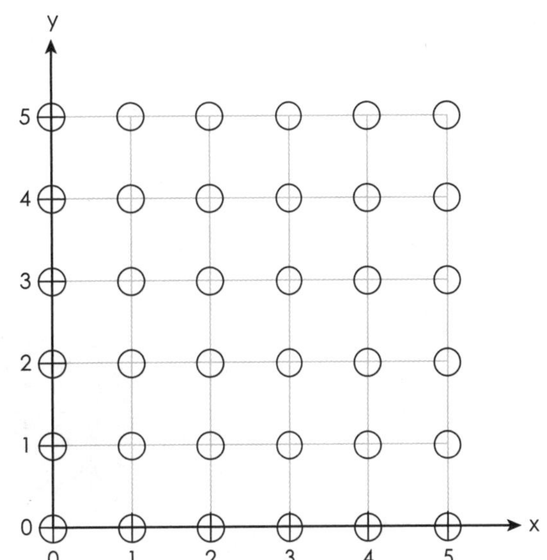

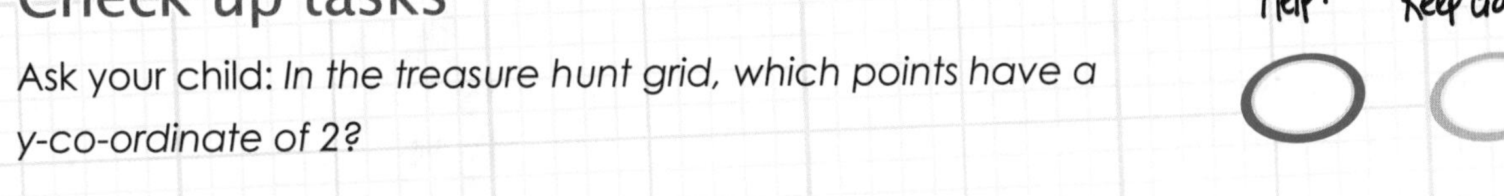

Check up tasks

Ask your child: *In the treasure hunt grid, which points have a y-co-ordinate of 2?*

Ask your child: *Look at grid A of question 3. If the 4th vertex was plotted at the point (8, 7), what shape would the four vertices make? In grid B draw the diagonals of the rectangle. What are the co-ordinates of the point at which they cross?*

Symmetry

Top Tip for Parents

In question 1 your child may have difficulty in identifying the line(s) of symmetry for some of the shapes. Ask your child to trace the shape on to blank paper, cut it out and test for symmetry by folding.

A mirror line is also called a line of symmetry or an axis of symmetry. A shape which can be divided into two matching halves has reflective symmetry.

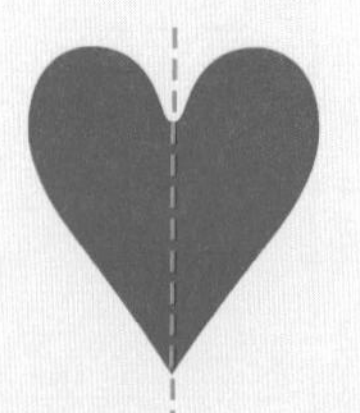

If you cut out a symmetrical shape and fold it along an axis of symmetry, one side will fit exactly on top of the other. A square has four lines of symmetry.

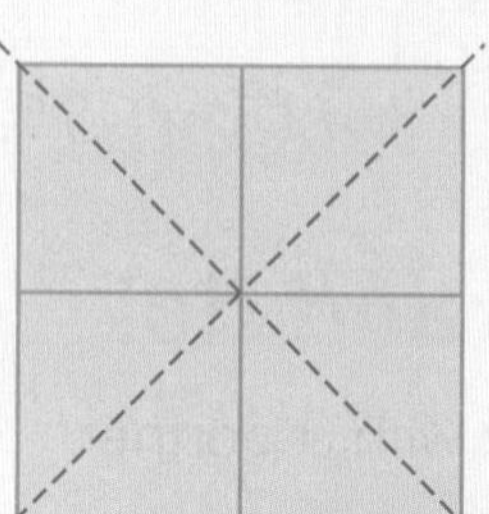

Exercises

1

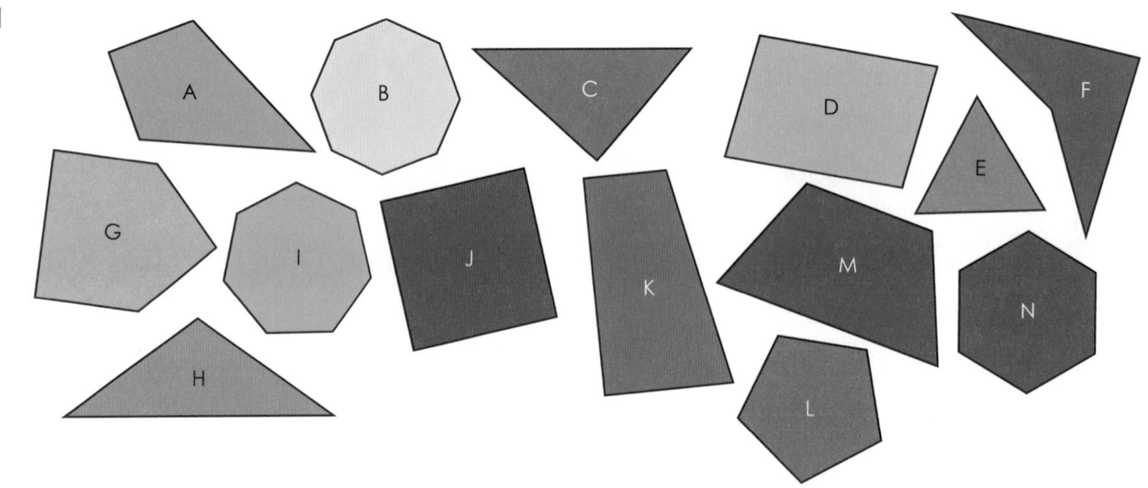

Write the letters of the 2D shapes that:

a do not have reflective symmetry; ________________

b have one line of symmetry; ________________

c have more than one line of symmetry. ________________

2 Reflect the shape first in the vertical axis of symmetry then reflect both shapes in the horizontal axis of symmetry. Colour the shape.

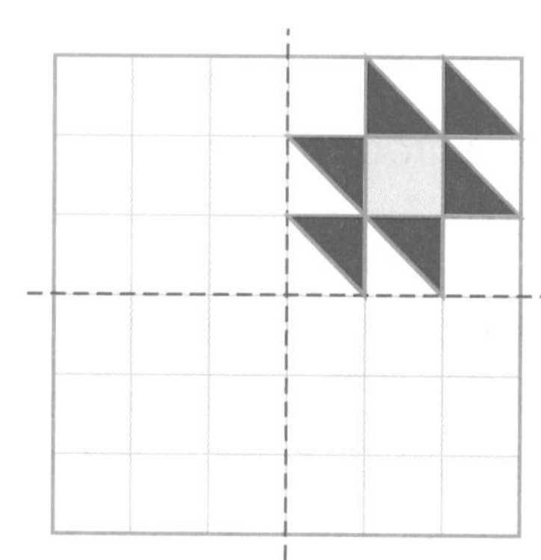

These shapes are drawn on 1 cm square dot paper.
For each shape, reflect it both ways in the diagonal axis of symmetry. Check that each pattern is symmetrical.

You need
- Ruler
- Coloured pens

a

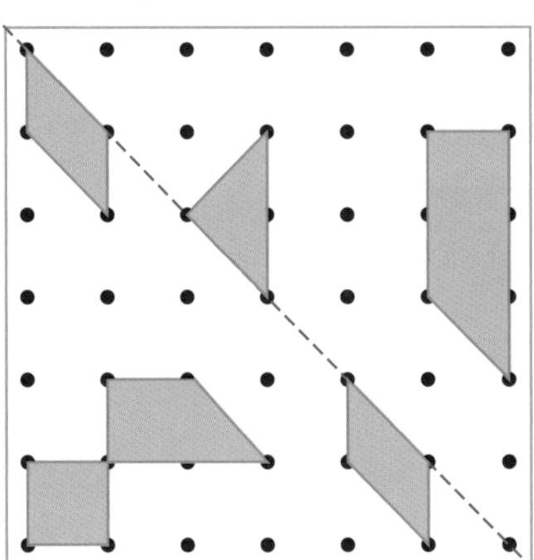

b

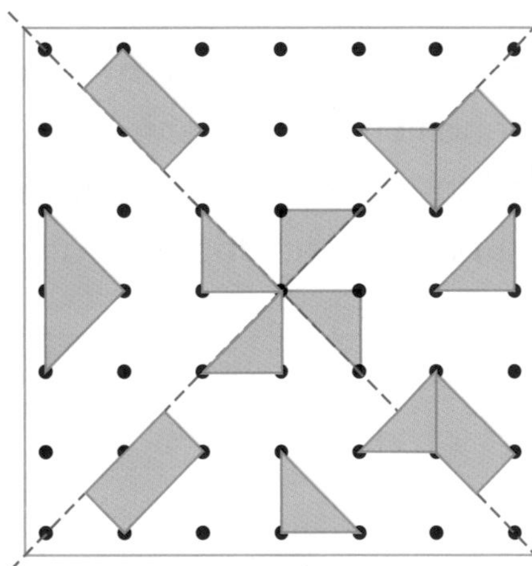

Go and do!

You need
- 1 cm squared paper
- Ruler
- Coloured pen

1 Mark out a 6 cm × 6 cm square on 1 cm squared paper. Draw the horizontal and vertical axes of symmetry. Design your own shape in the top right quarter and reflect it in both axes of symmetry. Colour your shape.

You need
- 1 cm squared paper
- Ruler
- Blue and red pens

2 How many different symmetrical designs can you make where three of the nine small squares are coloured blue?
   a Mark out 3 cm × 3 cm square grids on squared paper.
   b For each 3 cm × 3 cm square:
   - colour three small squares green and leave the rest blank;
   - mark the line of symmetry with a dotted red line.

   Reflections or rotations of the same design are not allowed.

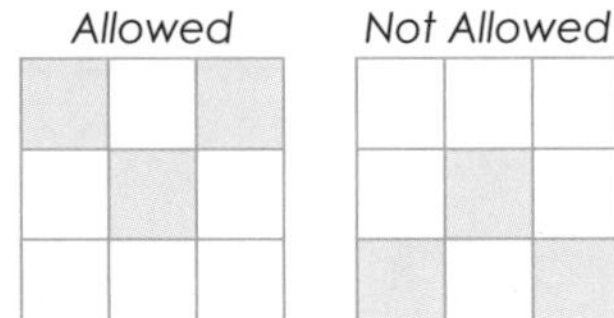

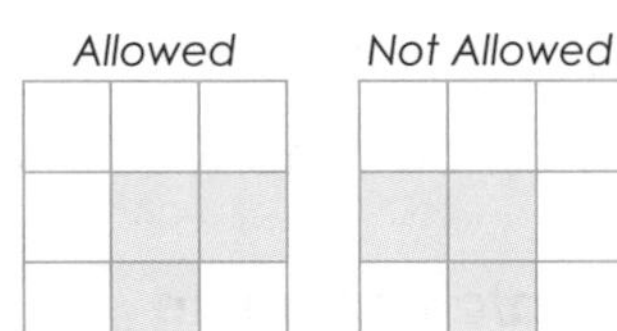

How did you do? All 10 possible designs – excellent
8–9 symmetrical designs – very good

Check up tasks

Ask your child: *What do you notice about the shapes in Exercises question 1 which have more than one axis of symmetry?*

Help! Keep Going! Good to go!

Data collection

We can collect small sets of data from surveys or questionnaires and from experiments. By presenting the data in various ways, e.g. simple frequency tables and bar charts, we can process and interpret the data and draw conclusions.

Top Tip for Parents

Check that your child records tally marks in fives, ||||, like four fingers and a thumb. This will make it easier to add the tally marks and enter the total in the frequency column.

Go and do!

Experiment 1 **Card game**

You need
- A pack of playing cards
- Two frequency tables

- Work with a partner. Remove the picture cards and jokers from a pack of cards. Shuffle the cards.
- Deal three cards to each player.
- Each player adds the card values to find a score and records the result in a frequency table.

Score	Tally	Frequency
1–5		
6–10		
11–15		
16–20		
21–25		
26–30		

Ace = 1

- Do this 20 times each.
- Compare your results with your partner's.
- Which scores have the highest frequency?

What if.... you made sets of four cards? Which scores would be most common?

Experiment 2 **Catching game**

You need
- 10 paper clips
- Two copies of the frequency table
- 1 cm squared paper

Is it easier to catch with your writing than your non-writing hand?

- Work in pairs. On your turn, place 10 paper clips on the back of your writing hand, toss them upwards, turn your hand and catch as many as you can.
- Repeat for your non-writing hand.
- Record your results in your frequency table.

Clips caught	1	2	3	4	5	6	7	8	9	10
Writing hand										
Non-writing hand										

- Repeat the experiment a further nine times.
- Compare your results with your partner's.
- Draw a bar chart for the data.

Experiment 3 **Investigating words and letters**

You need
- A favourite novel
- A calculator

- Work with a partner. Decide who will work with the book and who will record the tally marks.
- Choose a page at random. Count and mark off 100 consecutive words.
- Together complete the frequency table for the lengths of the words you have marked.
- Complete the bar chart to show your results.

Word length	Tally	Frequency
1–3		
4–6		
7–9		
10–12		
13+		

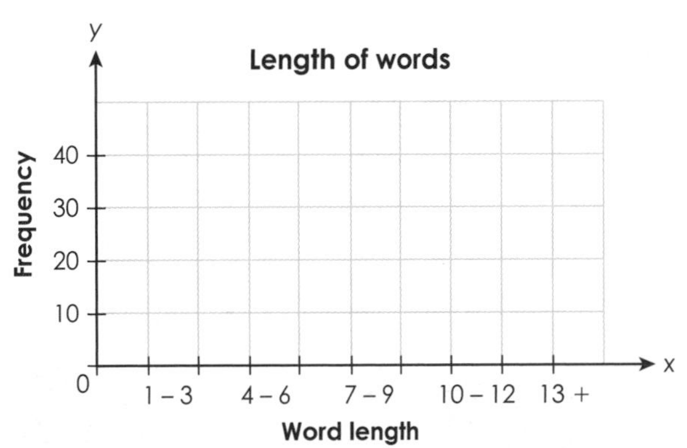

- What does the tallest bar show?
- If you repeat the experiment using a different source, e.g. a newspaper or magazine, will the results be the same?
- Using the same 100 consecutive words, record in the table the frequency with which different vowels occur.
- Convert the frequencies (F) to percentages (%).
- In Scrabble® 50% of the vowel tiles are either A or E and 50% are I, O or U. Compare your results with their frequency in Scrabble®.

Vowel	Tally	F	%
A			
E			
I			
O			
U			
Total Frequency			

Check up tasks

Ask your child: *Which is the most frequently used vowel in the English language?*

Ask your child: *Why is it sometimes useful to group data in equal class intervals?*

Pie charts

Pie charts are circular diagrams marked off into slices which make it easy for us to compare different amounts. In percentage pie charts the scale on the circumference is marked off and labelled in intervals of 10%.

Top Tip for Parents

If your child has difficulty in reading the scale on the percentage pie chart, ask him or her to count on in steps from one major division to the next in order to find what each small division represents.

Exercises

1 The table shows how some newspapers allocate space.

Title	Features	News	Sport	Other
Herald	30%	30%	25%	15%
Echo	20%	50%	25%	5%
Post	40%	25%	25%	10%

Work out which pie chart is for each paper and colour the key.

a

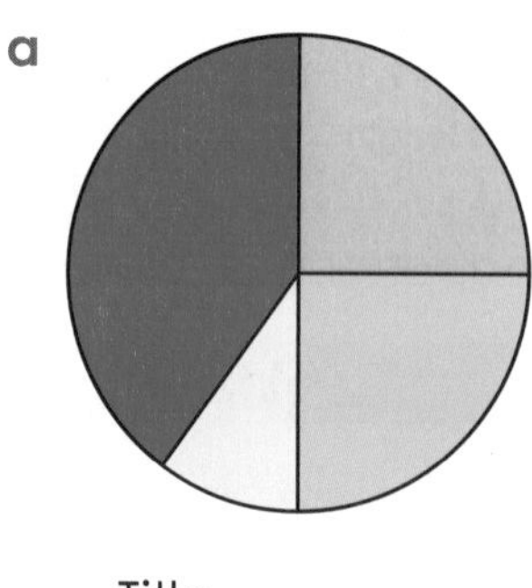

Title ___________

b

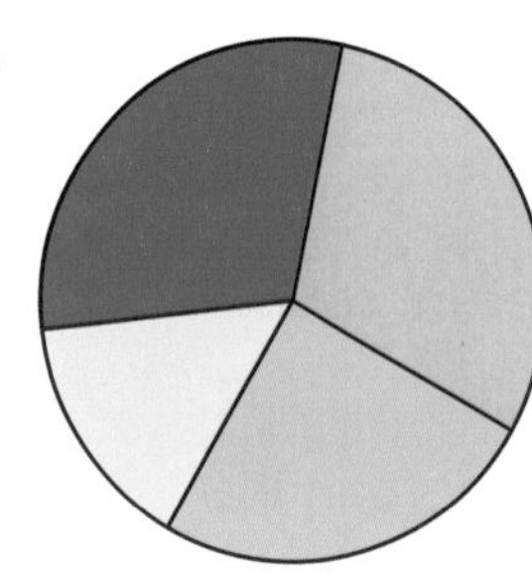

Title ___________

c

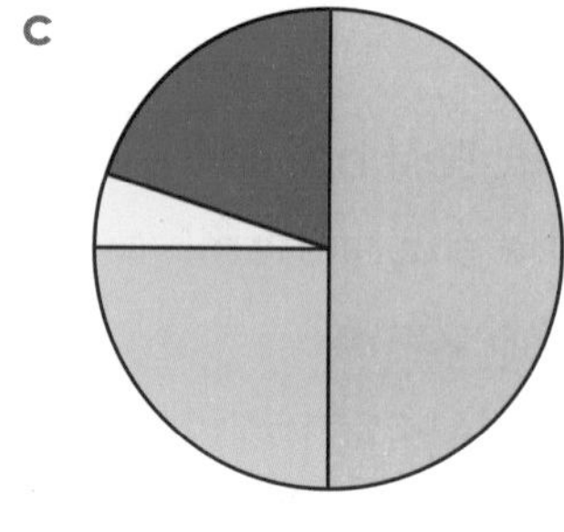

Title ___________

Key

Features	
News	
Sport	
Other	

2 **Dental health**

200 children, aged 11 to 12, took part in a survey about their dental health. Their answers are recorded in percentage pie charts. Use the pie charts to complete tables a, b and c.

a

When did you last visit your dental surgery?	Percentage of children	Number of children
a In the last 3 months		
b 3–6 months ago		
c More than 6 months ago		
d Over 1 year ago		

Date of last visit

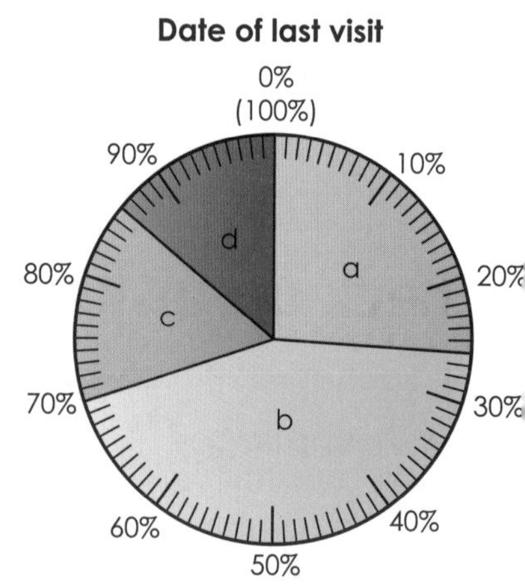

b

What was the reason for your last visit?	Percentage of children	Number of children
a in pain		
b regular check-up with dentist		
c filling or extraction		
d straightening teeth		

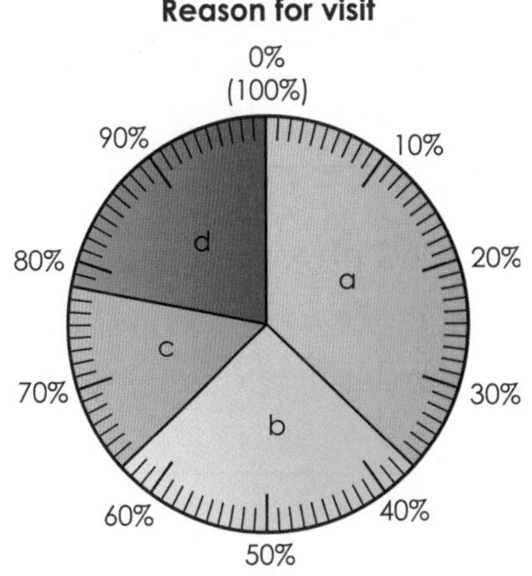

c

How often do you brush your teeth?	Percentage of children	Number of children
a less than once a day		
b once a day		
c twice a day		
d more than twice a day		

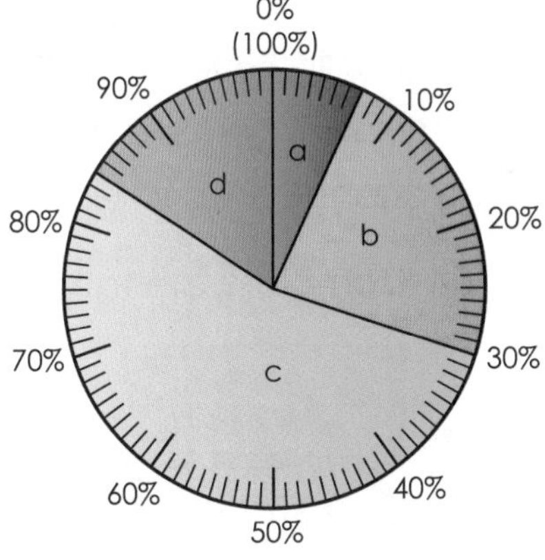

Go and do!

Dice scores Work with a partner

- Take it in turn to roll a 1–6 dice 25 times each.
- Make a frequency table to record each score.

Score	Tally	Frequency	%
1			
2			
3			
4			
5			
6			

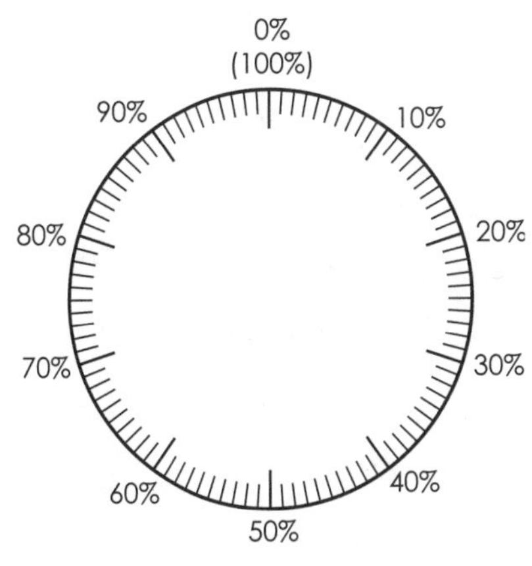

- Display your results in a pie chart

Check up tasks

Ask your child: *Look at the table in question 1. What clues did you find which helped you to match each pie chart to its newspaper title?*

Help! Keep Going! Good to go!

Conversion graphs

Top Tip for Parents

Check that your child does not choose a scale which produces a graph too small for accurate interpretation or too large to fit on to the squared or graph paper.

A conversion graph is a straight line graph used for converting a number of units to a different kind of unit, e.g. kilometres to miles, pounds (£) to dollars ($).

Exercises

You need

- Squared or graph paper

1 **Converting miles to kilometres**

5 miles is approximately equal to 8 kilometres, or 5 miles ≈ 8 km.

To change miles to kilometres, multiply by 8 and divide by 5.

a Complete the table of values.

Miles	0	5	10	15	20
Kilometres	0	8	16		
Co-ordinates	(0, 0)	(5, 8)			

b Plot each point on squared or graph paper. Join the points with a ruler and extend the straight line as far as it will go.

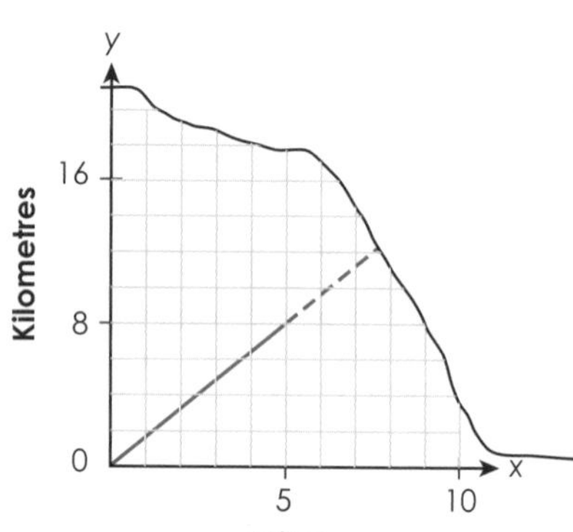

c Use your graph to find the equivalent distances.

45 miles ≈ _______ km 64 km ≈ _______ miles

75 miles ≈ _______ km 30 km ≈ _______ miles

d If 5 miles ≈ 8 km then 50 miles ≈ 80 km.

Convert these distances:

250 miles ≈ _______ km 350 miles ≈ _______ km 1010 miles ≈ _______ km

e Use the functions to convert these distances from Inverness.

miles → × 8 → ÷ 5 → km

km → × 5 → ÷ 8 → miles

Where needed, round your answers to the nearest mile or kilometre.

Distances from Inverness		
Town	miles	km
Aberdeen	103	
Ayr		320
Fort William	65	
Glasgow	168	
Ullapool		88
Thurso	110	

Go and do!

1 Converting pounds (£) to other currencies

A Scottish company manufactures and exports golfing goods worldwide. These are the retail prices in the UK for some of their products.

You need
- Squared or graph paper
- Calculator

a Find on BBC Teletext, page 240, Foreign Exchange, the current exchange rates for the currencies of:

i USA ii Germany

iii Australia iv South Africa

b Draw a conversion graph for each currency.

c Use the graph to calculate the retail price of each product sold in the four countries. Round the prices to the nearest dollar, euro or rand.

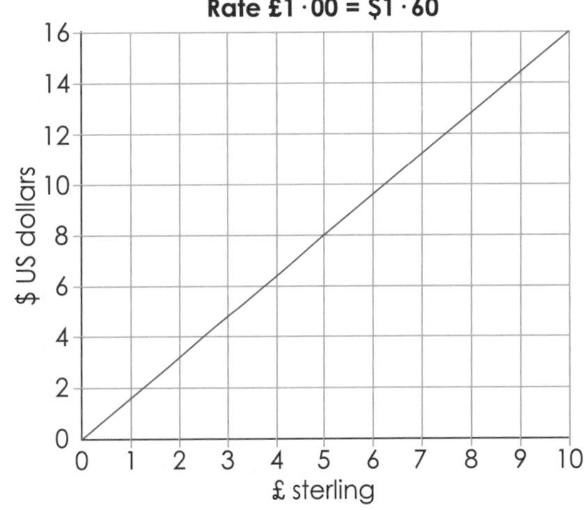

2 Converting temperatures from °C to °F.

You need
- Squared or graph paper

a Use this table of values to draw a conversion graph.

°C	0	5	10	16	28
°F	0	40	50	61	82

b On BBC Teletext, page 410, you will find the five-day forecast in °C for cities of the world. If you live in the United States, temperatures are always quoted in the media in °F. Choose 10 US cities. Convert the temperatures from °C to °F.

Check up tasks

Ask your child: *How many dollars ($) will you get for £100? How many euros (€)?*

Probability

> **Top Tip for Parents**
>
> Your child should be aware that an event which is more likely to happen is not always the actual outcome, i.e. what actually happens. This can be best demonstrated in a sporting event where the team or the contestant expected to win may actually lose.

Probability is about how likely or unlikely the outcome of an event is. We can measure the chance or likelihood of a particular outcome on a scale from 0 to 1, with the lowest probability at zero (impossible) and the highest probability at 1 (certain).

Example

In a bag of 6 sweets, 3 are coloured yellow, 2 are red and 1 is green.

If you take a sweet at random from the bag there is a 3 in 6 or even chance that the colour is yellow so the probability of choosing a yellow sweet is $\frac{3}{6}$ so $P(Y) = \frac{1}{2}$. It is less likely or a poor chance that your sweet is red, 2 in 6, so $P(R) = \frac{1}{3}$.

It is not possible to choose an orange coloured sweet from this bag so $P(O) = 0$. However if all 6 sweets in the bag are yellow then $P(Y) = 1$.

Exercises

1 **Nets of cubes**

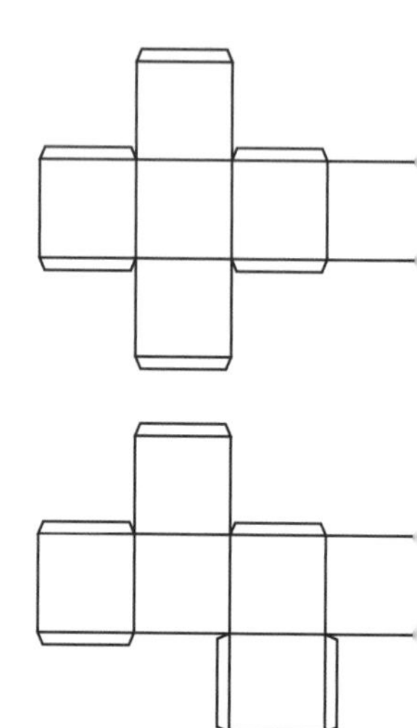

a Colour the net so that the assembled cube has an even chance of rolling red or blue.
The cube has □ red and □ blue faces.

b Colour this net so that there is a 1 in 3 chance of rolling red or blue or green.
The cube has □ red, □ blue and □ green faces.

c Imagine a cube with 1 red, 2 blue and 3 green faces. Complete the table for the chance and probability of rolling each colour.

Event	Chance	Probability
Red		
	2 in 6	
		$\frac{1}{2}$

2 ***Impossible*** ***Unlikely*** ***Even*** ***Likely*** ***Certain***

Choose one of the above words to describe the likelihood that the coin you take out of the purse is:

- copper
- silver
- heptagonal
- less than £2
- more than 5p
- is a 2p coin

Go and do!

1 Collect the 12 coins in question 2 and put them in a purse. Take at random a coin from the purse and record the event in a table. Return the coin to the purse and repeat the task four more times.

Event	Chance	Probability
£1	1 in 12	$\frac{1}{12}$

2 **Pin up, pin down** **An activity for two players**

a What is the probability of a drawing pin dropped on to your table landing point up? Tick you prediction.

	Less likely	Even chance	More likely
Player 1			
Player 2			

b **Experiment**

- Decide who will drop the pins and who will record.
- Put 10 drawing pins into the cup, shake and drop the pins on to the table.
- Record in the table how many pins land point up and point down.
- Repeat a further nine times.

You need
- Paper cup
- 10 drawing pins

	1	2	3	4	5	6	7	8	9	10	Total

c Compare the results of your experiment with your prediction.

Check up tasks

Ask your child: *There are 12 coins in a purse. 3 are copper and 9 are silver. What is the probability that the coin you take from the purse is copper? Is silver? Is £1?*

Place value in numbers

b 9 000 000 c 7000 d 500 000 e $\frac{8}{10}$ f $\frac{6}{100}$

b > c < d < e < f >

05 m b 34·69 m c 34·27 m

Go and do!

1 Open

2

2·401	2·402	2·403	2·404	2·405	2·406	2·407	2·408	2·409	2·410
2·411	2·412	2·413	2·414	2·415	2·416	2·417	2·418	2·419	2·420
2·421	2·422	2·423	2·424	2·425	2·426	2·427	2·428	2·429	2·430
2·431	2·432	2·433	2·434	2·435	2·436	2·437	2·438	2·439	2·440
2·441	2·442	2·443	2·444	2·445	2·446	2·447	2·448	2·449	2·450
2·451	2·452	2·453	2·454	2·455	2·456	2·457	2·458	2·459	2·460
2·461	2·462	2·463	2·464	2·465	2·466	2·467	2·468	2·469	2·470
2·471	2·472	2·473	2·474	2·475	2·476	2·477	2·478	2·479	2·480
2·481	2·482	2·483	2·484	2·485	2·486	2·487	2·488	2·489	2·490
2·491	2·492	2·493	2·494	2·495	2·496	2·497	2·498	2·499	2·5

The table shows that there are 99 3-place decimal numbers between 2·4 and 2·5.
The 80 3-place decimal numbers with one 4 are shown in black.
The 18 3-place decimal numbers with two 4s are shown in red.
The single 3-place decimal number with three 4s is shown in blue.

Pages 8–9 **Rounding and estimating**

1

	Number	To the nearest 10	To the nearest 100	To the nearest 1000
a	6985	6990	7000	7000
b	9658	9660	9700	10 000
c	56 098	56 100	56 100	56 000
d	68 905	68 910	68 900	69 000
e	650 981	650 980	651 000	651 000
f	605 189	605 190	605 200	605 000
g	1 986 506	1 986 510	1 986 500	1 987 000
h	1 869 519	1 869 520	1 869 500	1 870 000

2 a £6 b £8
c £3 d £13

3 a P ≈ 32 cm
b P ≈ 90 cm
c P ≈ 96 cm

Go and do! Open **Go and find!** Open

Pages 10–11 **In your head (1)**

1 a red 92, white 91, blue 93 b yellow 5·6, green 3·4, purple 35

c

Numbers	Total	Difference
Two highest whole numbers	156	26
Two lowest whole numbers	65	13
Two highest decimal numbers	15·7	1·3
Two lowest decimal numbers	6·7	0·9
Highest and lowest odd and whole numbers	130	52
Highest and lowest even and whole numbers	82	30

2 a

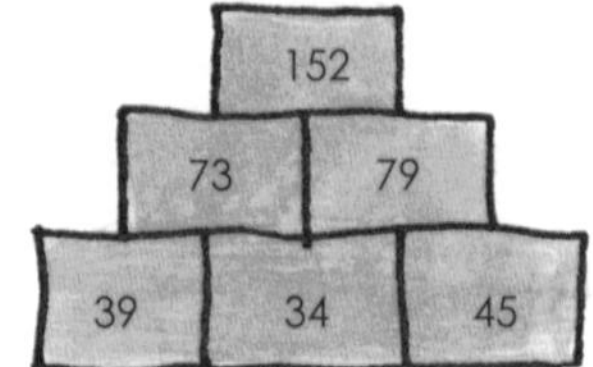

b

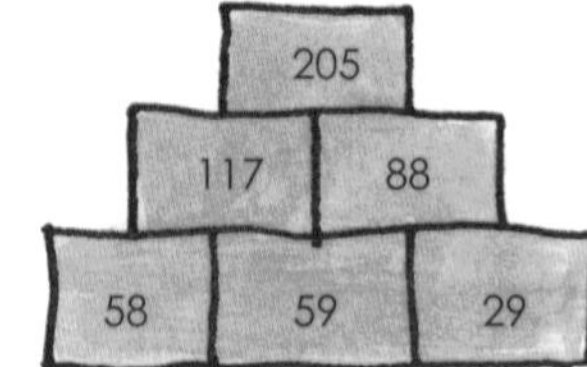

c

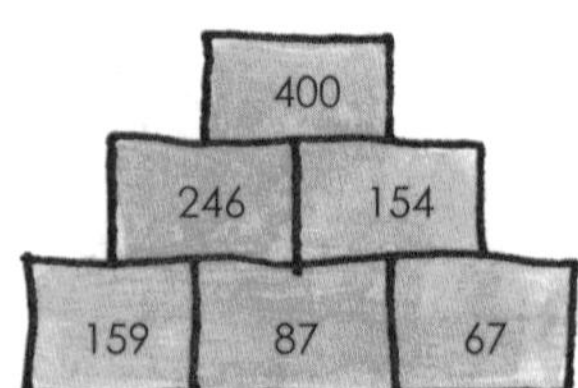

Go and do!

1 Largest total 169 Smallest total 165

2 Open

3 10 000, 9001, 8002, 7003, 6004, 5005, 4006, 3007, 2008, 1009, 10

ages 12–13 **Add and subtract**

a 8924 b 10 048 c 8219 d 21·76 e 46·34 f 158·16
g 4063 h 2058 i 6477 j 19·8 k 15·63 l 24·75

o and do!

, 2 Open

a 462 + 153 = 615 b 651 + 243 = 894 c 153 + 246 = 399 d 135 + 246 = 381

The missing line in a to d is 41976

a 11·1 − 1·11 = 9·99
22·2 − 2·22 = 19·98
33·3 − 3·33 = 29·97
44·4 − 4·44 = 39·96

b The difference between consecutive answers is 9·99 each time.
c Open
d The difference between consecutive answers is 109·989 each time.

ages 14–15 **In your head (2)**

Open

Buy	× £1·60
10	£16
100	£160
50	£80
25	£40

netballs @ £23 each

Buy	× £0·46
10	£4·60
100	£46
50	£23
60	£27·60

skittles @ £7·99 each

Buy	× £7·00
100	£700
500	£3500
250	£1750
400	£2800

softballs @ £16 each

footballs @ £35 each

o and do!

, 2 Open

Largest product: 42·4 Smallest product 17·4

ages 16–17 **Using brackets**

Possible answers are: 4, 10 and 42

a (4 × 6) − 8 = 16 b (4 × 6) ÷ 8 = 3 c 8 + (4 × 6) = 32 d 6 − (8 ÷ 4) = 4

a (12 + 3) + (4 + 5) = 24 or (12 ÷ 3) + (4 × 5) = 24 b (12 × 3) − (4 × 5) = 16
c (5 × 4) ÷ (3 + 2) + 1 = 5 d (5 + 43) − 21 = 27

a 8, 16, 32, 64, 128 b 15, 30, 60, 120, 240 c 23, 46, 92, 184, 368

a 648 b 3228 c 93·6

a 60 b 78 c 63 d 60 e 72 f 165

o and do!

Possible answers are: 84, 96 and 100

ages 18–19 **Multiplication methods**

a 498 b 235 c 2032 d 1521 e 3072 f 3003

a 198, 396, 594 b 495, 693, 891

a 200·2 b 300·3 c 400·4 d 500·5 e 700·7 f 900·9

o and do!

Open

13 × 11 × 7 = 1001 so any 3-digit number multiplied by 1001 will have its digits repeated in the answer.

ages 20–21 **Division methods**

a 26 b 42 c 55 d 28
e 74 f 48 g 66 h 52

a 16·4: 16 trays b 28·6: 28 trays c 59·5: 59 trays
d 70·8: 70 trays e 57·4: 57 trays f 120·9: 120 trays

o and do!

a 27 or 57 or 87 b 12 or 68

a 8)463 = 57R7 b 5)349 = 69R4 c 6)208·8 = 34·8

a 304 ÷ 4 = 76 b 585 ÷ 9 = 65

o and find! Open

Answers

Pages 22–23 **Divisibility**

1 b by 3 501, 504, 507, 510, 513, 516, 519, 522, 525, 528, 531, 534, 537, 540, 543, 546, 549
by 4 504, 508, 512, 516, 520, 524, 528, 532, 536, 540, 544, 548
c by 6 504, 510, 516, 522, 528, 534, 540, 546
by 8 504, 512, 520, 528, 536, 544
by 6 and 8 504, 528
d by 12 504, 516, 528, 540

2 a green b red c green d red
e red f green g red h green

3 by 7 504, 511, 518, 525, 532, 539, 546

Go and do! Open

Pages 24–25 **Patterns and puzzles**

1 Table ○: 6 times table Table △: 9 times table

2 a, b

1	3	5	7	9	11	13
2	6	10	14	18	22	26
4	12	20	28	36	44	52
8	24	40	56	72	88	104
16	48	80	112	144	176	208

c Row 1: add 2, Row 2: add 4
Row 3: add 8, Row 4: add 16
d Double the previous number.
e Every number between 1 and 100 appears without duplication.

3 a $12 \times 99 = 1188$
$23 \times 99 = 2277$
$34 \times 99 = 3366$
$45 \times 99 = 4455$
$56 \times 99 = 5544$

b $8 \times 1 + 1 = 9$
$8 \times 12 + 2 = 98$
$8 \times 123 + 3 = 987$
$8 \times 1234 + 4 = 9876$
$8 \times 12345 + 5 = 98765$

4 a Open
b Rule works for 3-digit consecutive numbers.
c 89, 144. Rule applies to numbers in Fibonacci sequence.

Go and find! Open

Pages 26–27 **Common factors and multiples**

1

Multiples of 3	3	6	9	12	15	18	21	24	27	30
Multiples of 4	4	8	12	16	20	24	28	32	36	40
Multiples of 5	5	10	15	20	25	30	35	40	45	50

2 a 12, 24 b 15, 30 c 20, 40

3 a 36, 48, 60, 72, 84 b 45, 60, 75, 90, 105 c 60, 80, 100, 120, 140

4 a 24 b 12 c 18 d 42 e 36 f 60

5 a 1, 2, 4, 5, 8, 10, 20, 40 b 1, 2, 4, 8, 16, 32, 64 c 1, 2, 3, 5, 6, 9, 10, 15, 18, 30, 45, 90

6 a

					24		30		40			
					12		15	36	20		64	
		12		18	8		10	18	10		32	
		6	16	9	6		6	12	8		16	81
		4	8	6	4		5	6	5		8	27
4	9	3	4	3	3	25	3	3	4	49	4	9
2	3	2	2	2	2	5	2	2	2	7	2	3
1	1	1	1	1	1	1	1	1	1	1	1	1
4	9	12	16	18	24	25	30	36	40	49	64	81

b i Even number of factors: 12, 18, 24, 30, 40, 90 ii Odd number of factors: 4, 9, 16, 25, 36, 49, 64, 81
c Square numbers

Go and do! Open

ages 28–29 **Negative differences**

Open

Temperature in °C	Sun	Mon	Tues	Wed	Thur	Fri	Sat
Maximum temperature	3°	0°	−2°	−3°	4°	1°	5°
Minimum temperature	−4°	−9°	−10°	−13°	−6°	−5°	−1°
Difference	7°	9°	8°	10°	10°	6°	6°

a

−2	−9	−4
−7	−5	−3
−6	−1	−8

b

−9	−10	−5
−4	−8	−12
−11	−6	−7

c

5	0	4	−7
−5	2	−2	7
−6	3	−1	6
8	−3	1	−4

d

0	1	7	−6
4	−3	−5	6
−7	8	2	−1
5	−4	−2	3

o and do! Open

ages 30–31 **Simply fractions**

a i $\frac{1}{5} = \frac{2}{10}, \frac{3}{15}, \frac{4}{20}, \frac{5}{25}, \frac{6}{30}, \frac{7}{35}\ \frac{8}{40}, \frac{9}{45}, \frac{10}{50}$ ii $\frac{1}{3} = \frac{2}{6}, \frac{3}{9}, \frac{4}{12}, \frac{5}{15}, \frac{6}{18}, \frac{7}{21}, \frac{8}{24}, \frac{9}{27}, \frac{10}{30}$

b Open

c i $\frac{2}{7}$ ii $\frac{1}{2}$ iii $\frac{3}{4}$ iv $\frac{3}{8}$ v $\frac{1}{3}$ vi $\frac{3}{10}$ vii $\frac{1}{2}$ viii $\frac{2}{3}$

a $\frac{2}{3}$ red, $\frac{1}{3}$ not red b $\frac{3}{5}$ red, $\frac{2}{5}$ not red

c $\frac{1}{4}$ red, $\frac{3}{4}$ not red d $\frac{5}{12}$ red, $\frac{7}{12}$ not red

a $\frac{3}{10}, \frac{2}{5}, \frac{1}{2}$ b $\frac{1}{4}, \frac{5}{16}, \frac{3}{8}$ c $\frac{2}{5}, \frac{9}{20}, \frac{7}{10}$ d $\frac{3}{5}, \frac{7}{10}, \frac{5}{6}$

e $\frac{5}{6}, \frac{7}{8}, \frac{11}{12}$ f $\frac{1}{2}, \frac{5}{8}, \frac{2}{3}, \frac{3}{4}$ g $\frac{1}{2}, \frac{3}{4}, \frac{7}{9}, \frac{5}{6}$

o and do!

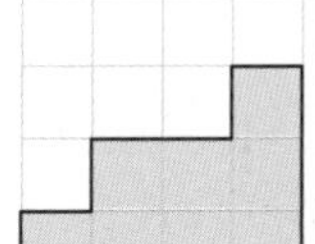
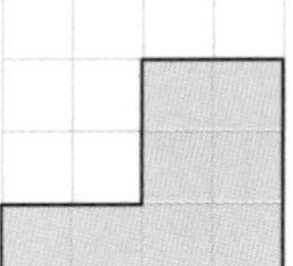
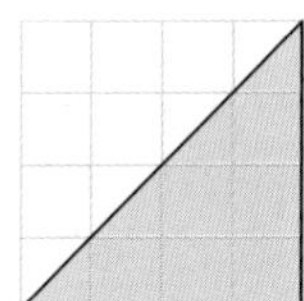
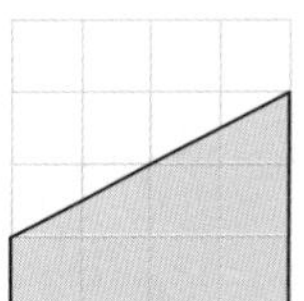

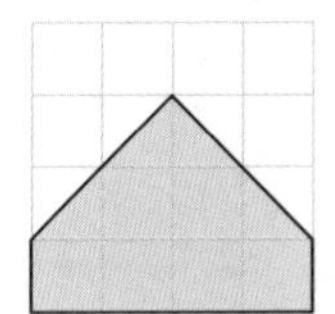
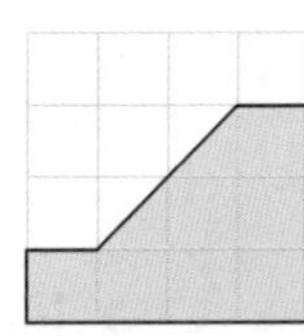
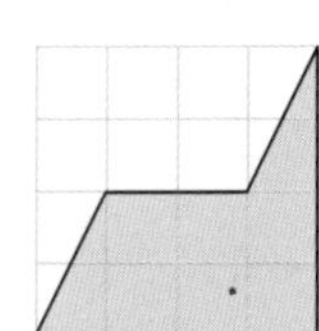
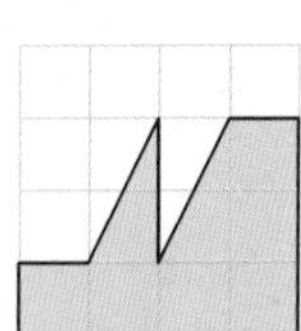

Open

$\frac{1}{2} = \frac{18}{36}, \frac{24}{48}, \frac{36}{72}, \frac{48}{96}$ $\frac{2}{3} = \frac{24}{36}, \frac{36}{54}, \frac{48}{72}, \frac{64}{96}$ $\frac{3}{4} = \frac{18}{24}, \frac{36}{48}\ \frac{48}{64}, \frac{54}{72}, \frac{72}{96}$

ages 32–33 **Finding percentages**

b

Multiple	No. of squares with a cross	% of squares with a cross
2	50	50%
3	33	33%
5	20	20%

c 26%

Answers

2 a

Amount	50%	25%	75%
36	18	9	27
76	38	19	57
180	90	45	135
220	110	55	165
460	230	115	345
940	470	235	705
1120	560	280	840

b

Amount	10%	20%	5%	30%
£72	£7·20	£14·40	£3·60	£21·60
£25	£2·50	£5	£1·25	£7·50
£66	£6·60	£13·20	£3·30	£19·80
£84	£8·40	£16·80	£4·20	£25·20
£160	£16	£32	£8	£48
£350	£35	£70	£17·50	£105
£1200	£120	£240	£60	£360

Go and do!

1 Open

2 a The ball rises 1·28 m b After the 5th bounce

Go and find!

1 a Burj Khalifa in Dubai at 828 m
b 21·1968 m c After the 7th bounce

Pages 34–35 **What's the equivalence?**

1

Fraction	$\frac{4}{5}$	$\frac{7}{10}$	$\frac{2}{5}$	$\frac{3}{4}$	$\frac{3}{8}$	$\frac{2}{3}$	$\frac{11}{20}$
Decimal	0·8	0·7	0·4	0·75	0·375	0·667	0·55
Percentage	80%	70%	40%	75%	$37\frac{1}{2}$%	$66\frac{2}{3}$%	55%

2 a 30% b 40% c 28% d $12\frac{1}{2}$%

3 a

5p coin	10p coin	20p coin	50p coin	£1 coin	£2 coin
Fraction	$\frac{1}{2}$	$\frac{1}{4}$	$\frac{1}{10}$	$\frac{1}{20}$	$\frac{1}{40}$
Decimal	0·5	0·25	0·1	0·05	0·025
Percentage	50%	25%	10%	5%	$2\frac{1}{2}$%

b

2p coin	5p coin	10p coin	20p coin	50p coin	£1 coin	£2 coin
Fraction	$\frac{2}{5}$	$\frac{1}{5}$	$\frac{1}{10}$	$\frac{2}{50}$	$\frac{2}{100}$	$\frac{2}{200}$
Decimal	0·4	0·2	0·1	0·04	0·02	0·01
Percentage	40%	20%	10%	4%	2%	1%

Go and do!

1

Description	Fraction	Decimal (to 2 dec. places)	Percentage (to nearest whole number)
Is a double	$\frac{1}{4}$	0·25	25%
Sum of the dots is greater than 6	$\frac{3}{7}$	0·43	43%
With at least one even number	$\frac{9}{14}$	0·64	64%
Does not have a blank	$\frac{3}{4}$	0·75	75%
Difference is an odd number	$\frac{3}{7}$	0·43	43%

2 a

Fraction	$\frac{21}{30}$	$\frac{36}{72}$	$\frac{2}{5}$	$\frac{6}{60}$	$\frac{14}{16}$	$\frac{18}{24}$	$\frac{23}{50}$	$\frac{9}{36}$	$\frac{1}{8}$
Decimal	0·3	0·5	0·6	0·9	0·125	0·25	0·54	0·75	0·875

b Open

Pages 36–37 **Fractions and percentages**

1 a 4·5 kg b 10 kg c 13·5 kg
d 17·5 kg e 31·5 kg

2 a 150 ml b 480 ml c 1800 ml
d 100 ml e 3750 ml

3 a £78 b £32·40 c £69·60 d £420

4 a £31·50 b £75·20 c £22·50
d £14 e £38·50 f £59·50

5 $\frac{1}{10}$

Go and do!
1, 2 Open

Pages 38–39 **Manage money**

1 a

Shopping list	Special offer cost	Shelf price cost
6 morning rolls	£0·90	£1·20
3 peppers	£1·50	£1·65
400 g bacon	£4·95	£5·20
12 large eggs	£3·80	£3·25
4 cans beans	£1·00	£1·16
240 tea bags	£3·87	£3·45

b

Shopping list	Cost	Saving
6 morning rolls	£0·90	30p
3 peppers	£1·50	15p
400 g bacon	£4·95	25p
12 large eggs	£3·25	55p
4 cans beans	£1·00	16p
240 tea bags	£3·45	42p
Total	£15·50	£1·83

2 Lochside is £1 cheaper

3 a £19 b £17 c £18
d £27 e £20 f £22·50
g £63 h £70 i £60 j £3

4 Simon: June Amy: October Vera: September Eddie: December

Go and find! Open

Pages 40–41 **Profit and loss**

1

Type of refreshment	Percentage of refreshment	Profit
Popcorn	30%	£150
Soft drinks	15%	£75
Ice cream	35%	£175
Sweets	20%	£100

2 Alex: £3·60 Beth: £6·25 Colin: £6·40
Diana: £19·50 Emma and Frank: £20·35

3 Josef: £80 Kim: £120 Len: £150 Marie: £50 Nafisa: £125

4 a £1100 b £900 c £1500 d £700
e £1250 f £850 g £1650

Go and find! Open

Pages 42–43 **Times and events**

1 a

Depart Heathrow	07:15	08:55	11:50	14:20	16:05	18:20	20:20
Arrive Aberdeen	08:45	10:25	13:20	15:50	17:35	19:50	21:50

b Depart at 14:35. Arrive at 16:05.
c About 3 hours

2 a 55 min b 25 min c 0803 train
d 0734 – change at Linlithgow. 0749 – Change at Lenzie.

3 a 0950 train from Glasgow Central b At 9:00 am approx.
c i

	Red Team			Blue Team		
	1 Alex	2 Ben	3 Kim	1 Derek	2 Flo	3 Pat
Start time	2:30 pm	2:30 pm	2:30 pm	2:30 pm	2:30 pm	2:30 pm
Running time	50 min	55 min	62 min	58 min	47 min	64 min
Finishing time	3:20 pm	3:25 pm	3:32 pm	3:28 pm	3:17 pm	3:34 pm

ii Red team: 2 hr 47 min Blue team: 2 hr 49 min
iii Runner 1 - 48 min, Runner 2 - 52 min, Runner 3 - 65 min.

Go and do!
1 Open

2 18 times : 01:23, 01:32, 02:13, 02:31, 03:12, 03:21, 10:23, 10:32, 12:03, 12:30, 13:02, 13:20, 20:13, 20:31, 21:03, 21:30, 23:01, 23:10

Pages 44–45 **Time, speed and distance**

1 a 1·5 hrs b 2 hrs c 3 hrs d 4·5 hrs

2 a 60 km/h b 50 km/h c 500 km/h d 60 km/h

3 a 120 miles b 3500 miles c 210 miles d 4 miles

4 a i 15 miles ii 25 miles iii 40 miles

b i $1\frac{1}{4}$ hours ii $\frac{3}{4}$ hour

c 4 pm

Go and do! Open

Pages 46–47 **Units of measurement**

1

Line	Length in cm	Length in mm	Length in m
Zero to A	1·2 cm	12 mm	0·012 m
Zero to B	2·7 cm	27 mm	0·027 m
Zero to C	4·6 cm	46 mm	0·046 m
Zero to D	7·9 cm	79 mm	0·079 m
Zero to E	9·8 cm	98 mm	0·098 m
Zero to F	11·3 cm	113 mm	0·113 m

2 a 9200 g, 9·2 kg b 11 900 g, 11·9 kg
c 10 600 g, 10·6 kg d 7800 g, 7·8 kg
e 9100 g, 9·1 kg f 168 g, 0·168 kg

3

Level	Millilitres	Centilitres	Litres
a	170 ml	17 cl	0·17 ℓ
b	330 ml	33 cl	0·33 ℓ
c	500 ml	50 cl	0·5 ℓ
d	670 ml	67 cl	0·67 ℓ
e	840 ml	84 cl	0·84 ℓ
f	910 ml	91 cl	0·91 ℓ

Go and do!
1 a girl 32 kg b boy 41 kg c Sandy 12 kg

Coin	Diameter	Weight	Thickness
£1	22·5 mm	9·5 g	3·15 mm
10p	24·5 mm	6·5 g	2·03 mm

a, c Open

b 0·1 km or 100 000 mm ÷ 24·5 mm = 4081·6 coins to 1 dec. place, 4081 × 10p = £408·10

Pages 48–49 **Perimeter and area**

1 a P = 24 cm, A = 32 cm^2
b P = 20 cm, A = 21 cm^2
c P = 20 cm, A = 25 cm^2
d P = 24 cm, A = 35·75 cm^2

2 a 44 cm b 72 cm c 74 cm

3 a 90 cm^2 b 180 cm^2 c 250 cm^2

4 a 54 cm^2 b 52 cm^2

Go and do!

1 Open

2 a 32 cm^2 b 12·5 cm^2 c 16 cm^2 d 30 cm^2 e 12 cm^2

Pages 50–51 **Volume**

1 8 cm^3, 16 cm^3, 24 cm^3

2 9 cm^3, 18 cm^3, 27 cm^3

3 a 120 cm^3 b 252 cm^3 c 225 cm^3

4 a h = 2 cm b l = 6 cm c b = 12 cm
d h = 9 cm e l = 4 cm f b = 10 cm

Go and do!

1 Open

2 Water level remains the same each time.

Pages 52–53 **Square and triangular numbers**

1 a

Term	1st	2nd	3rd	4th	5th	6th	7th	8th	9th	10th
Counting number	1	2	3	4	5	6	7	8	9	10
Square number	1	4	9	16	25	36	49	64	81	100

b

Index notation	2^2	7^2	9^2	8^2	3^2	5^2	12^2	11^2	4^2	6^2
Square number	4	49	81	64	9	25	144	121	16	36

2 a $5^2 + 5 = 30$ b $7^2 + 7 = 56$ c $12^2 + 6 = 150$ d $9^2 + 21 = 102$
e $8^2 - 12 = 52$ f $10^2 - 41 = 59$ g $6^2 - 28 = 8$ h $11^2 - 19 = 102$
i $3^2 + 5^2 = 34$ j $9^2 + 4^2 = 97$ k $8^2 - 7^2 = 15$ l $10^2 - 6^2 = 64$

3

Term	1st	2nd	3rd	4th	5th	6th	7th	8th	9th	10th
Triangular number	1	3	6	10	15	21	28	36	45	55
Difference	–	2	3	4	5	6	7	8	9	10

Go and do!

1 a $2^2 - 1^2 = 3$ b $3^2 - 2^2 = 5$ c $4^2 - 3^2 = 7$
d $5^2 - 4^2 = 9$ e $6^2 - 5^2 = 11$ f $7^2 - 6^2 = 13$

Pattern: The difference between two consecutive square numbers is the sum of these two numbers.

g $20^2 - 19^2 = 39$ h $45^2 - 44^2 = 89$ i $99^2 - 98^2 = 197$

2 a

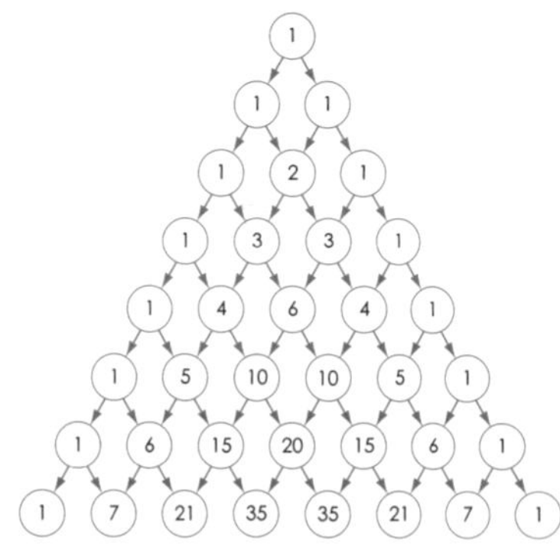

Total
1
2
4
8
16
32
64
128

b Each total is double the previous total
c 1, 3, 6, 10, 15, 21
d 256

Pages 54–55 **Matchstick puzzles**

Go and do!

1 a

Pattern number (P)	1	2	3	4	5	6	7
Number of matches (M)	6	11	16	21	26	31	36

M = (P × 5) + 1 or M = 5P + 1
a 36 b 51 c 101

b

Pattern number (P)	1	2	3	4	5	6	7
Number of matches (M)	5	12	19	26	33	40	47

M = (P × 7) − 2 or M = 7P − 2
a 47 b 68 c 138

c

Pattern number (P)	1	2	3	4	5	6	7
Number of matches (M)	7	12	17	22	27	32	37

M = (P × 5) + 2 or M = 5P + 2
a 37 b 52 c 102

d

Pattern number (P)	1	2	3	4	5	6	7
Number of matches (M)	5	10	15	20	25	30	35

M = (P × 5) or M = 5P
a 35 b 50 c 100

2 a

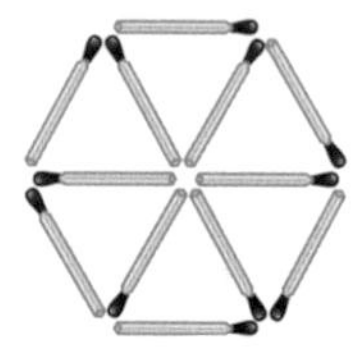

b

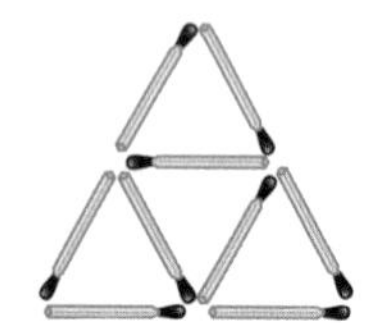

3

Pattern number (P)	1	2	3	4	5	6	7
Number of matches (M)	3	7	11	15	19	23	27

M = (P × 4) − 1 or M = 4P − 1
Pattern 25 = 99 struts

Pages 56–57 **Letters for numbers**

1 a = 1, b = 2, c = 3, d = 4, e = 5, f = 6, g = 7, h = 8

2 a 10 b 6 c 17 d 4
e 21 f 100 g 18 h 9

3 a 34 b 69 c 78 d 24
e 8 + 9 = 17 f 80 − 25 = 55 g 20 × 8 = 160

4 a k = 27 b l = 40 c m = 22

Go and do!

1 and 2 Open

Answers

Pages 58–59 **Expressions and equations**

1

Word statement	Expression
Add 5 to a number	$n + 5$
Subtract 6 from a number	$n - 6$
Subtract n from 8 or 8 minus n	$8 - n$
6 times a number	$6n$
8 divided by a number	$8 \div n$
Multiply a number by 5 and then take away 2	$5n - 2$
Divide a number by 4 and add 1	$(n \div 4) + 1$
Subtract 5 from a number and multiply the answer by 4	$4(n - 5)$
Add 6 to a number then multiply the answer by 8	$8(n + 6)$

2 a 28 b 47 c 48 d 60

3 a 300 m b 480 m c 720 m d 1200 m

Go and do!

1 a $a = 5$, $b = 3$, $c = 1$

2	7	6
9	5	1
4	3	8

b $a = 7$, $b = 3$, $c = 1$

10	3	8
5	7	9
6	11	4

Go and find! Open

Pages 60–61 **Classify 2D shapes**

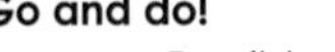

Go and do!

1 a Possible solution

1 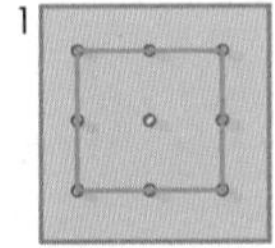
2 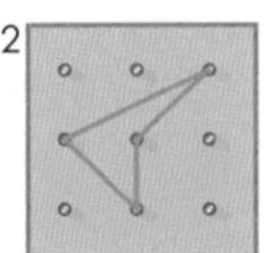
3 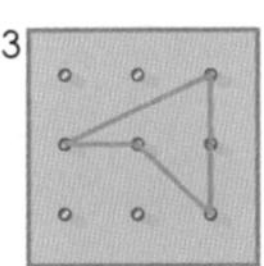
4 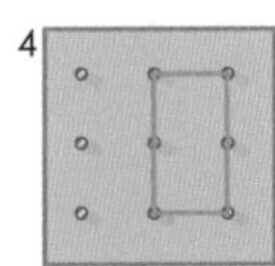
5 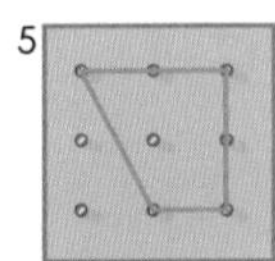
6 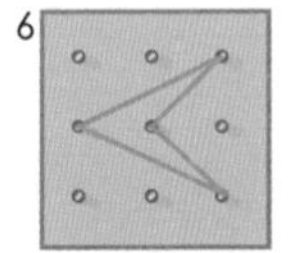
7 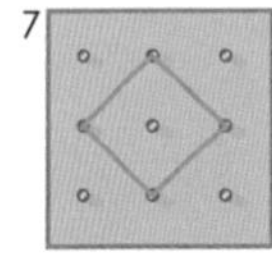
8 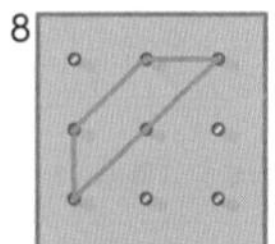

9 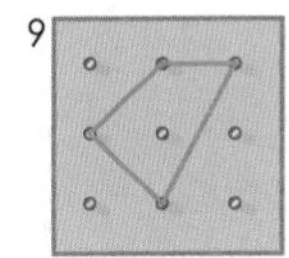
10 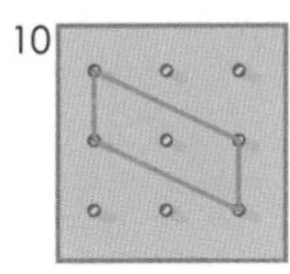
11 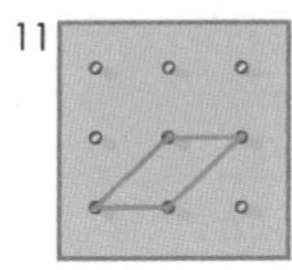
12 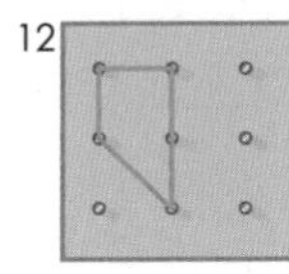
13 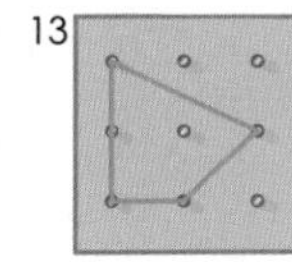
14 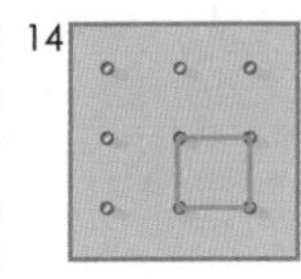
15 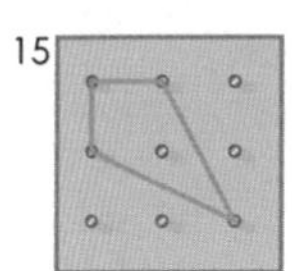
16 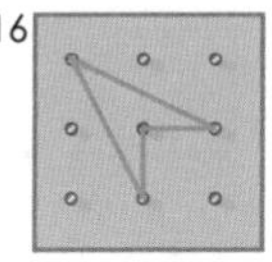

b Answers to match possible solution in 1a.
At least one line of symmetry – 1, 4, 6, 7, 8, 14, 15, 16
No pairs of parallel lines – 2, 3, 6, 9, 13, 15, 16
An interior angle greater than 180° – 2, 3, 6, 16

2, 3 Open

Pages 62–63 **Draw 2D shapes accurately**

1 b AB = 6·8 cm BC = 7·4 cm CA = 10 cm
FE = 3·4 cm DF = 3·7 cm ED = 5 cm

c Perimeter of △ ABC = 24·2 cm Perimeter of △ DEF = 12·1 cm

d Perimeter of outer triangle is twice that of the inner triangle.

2 e, f The lengths of pairs of parallel sides for the outer rectangle and outer rhombus are twice that of the inner rectangle and inner rhombus.

Go and do!

1

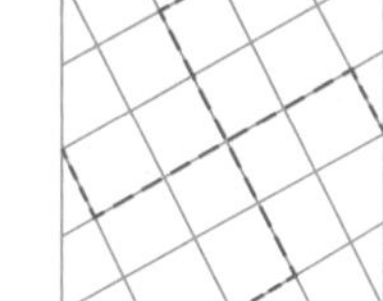

2 a square with shapes E, D and B
Perimeter ≈ 23 cm (allow ± 0·2 cm)
Area = 32 cm²

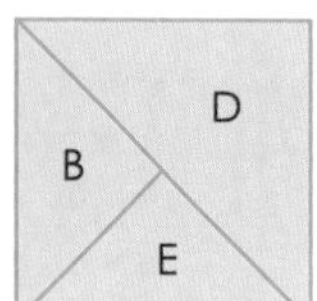

b hexagon with all 5 shapes
Perimeter ≈ 30·6 cm
(allow ± 0·2 cm)
Area = 64 cm²

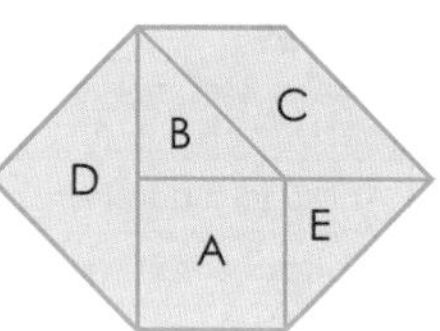

3 a

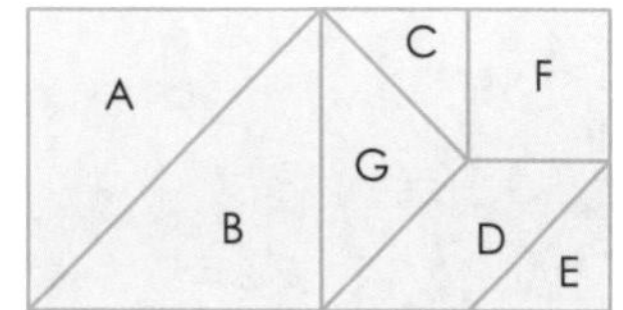

b

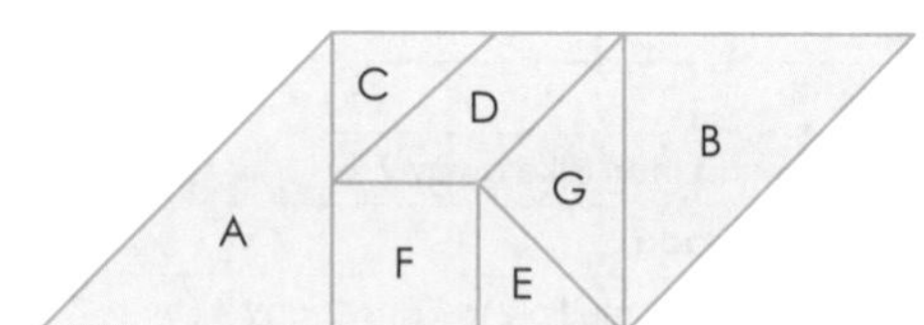

Pages 64–65 **Classify 3D solids**

1 a cube b hexagonal-based prism c square-based pyramid
d octahedron e cuboid f tetrahedron
g dodecahedron h triangular prism i pentagonal prism
j heptagonal-based pyramid

2 a

3D shape	Number of			
	Horizontal		Vertical	
	Faces	Edges	Faces	Edges
Pack of butter	2	8	4	4
Block of cheese	2	6	3	3
Packet of oatcakes	2	12	6	6

b AB // DC T PS // QR T XY // ZY F
DC ⊥CB T SR ⊥ PQ F WX ⊥WZ T

Go and do!

1 Open

2 Correct

3 a, b

Skeletal cube	Number of cubes	Difference
3 × 3 × 3	20	0
4 × 4 × 4	32	12
5 × 5 × 5	44	12
6 × 6 × 6	56	12

Pages 66–67 **Nets of 3D objects**

Go and do!

1, **2**, **3** and **4** Open

Pages 68–69 **Measure and calculate angles**

1 a 25° b 110° c 90° d 70°
e 45° f 135° g 70°

2 a ∠D = 50° ∠E = 75° ∠F = 55°
b 180°

3 a ∠P = 49° b ∠Q = 36°

4 ∠a = 325° ∠b = 231° ∠c = 205° ∠d = 73°

Go and do!

1 a 60° b 150° c 300°

2 a 15° b 105° c 225°

Pages 70–71 **Drawing angles**

1 Open

2 a ∠B = 50°, ∠C = 50°. b ∠L = 40°, ∠M = 75°.

3 a AC = 6·7 cm, BC = 7 cm, ∠C = 65°
b DF = 5·5 cm, EF = 9 cm, ∠F = 35°

4 Vertically opposite angles are equal and measure 77° and 103°.

Go and do!
At each bank of the river the angles made by the bridge are ≈ 60° and ≈120°.

Pages 72–73 **Reasoning about lines and angles**

1 a PS // QR SR = PQ
b ∠PQR and ∠RPQ

2

Diagram	∠X	∠Y	∠Z
a	35°	45°	100°
b	160°	160°	20°
c	105°	145°	110°
d	60°	60°	120°
e	23°	23°	67°

Go and do!
1 ∠a = 36°, ∠b = 72°, ∠c = 108°
2 Open
3 4

Pages 74–75 **Compass points, maps and plans**

1 a 135° b 135° c 225°

2 a NW b SW c W d S

Go and do! Open

Go and find! Open

Pages 76–77 **Co-ordinates**

1 a A (0, 5), B (3, 4), C (1, 3), D (6, 3), E (2, 2), F (8, 2), G (3, 1), H (10, 1)
b

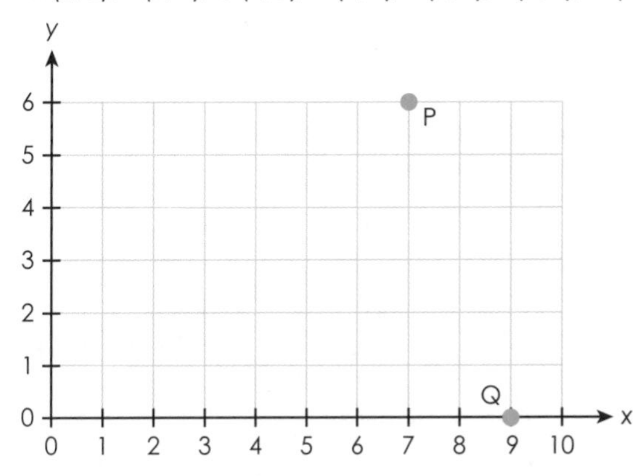

2 4th vertex Grid A (6, 7) Grid B (8, 3)

Go and do!
1 Open

Pages 78–79 **Symmetry**

1 a None: C, D, K b One: A, F, G, H, M
c More than 1: B, E, I, J, L, N – all are regular pentagons

2 a

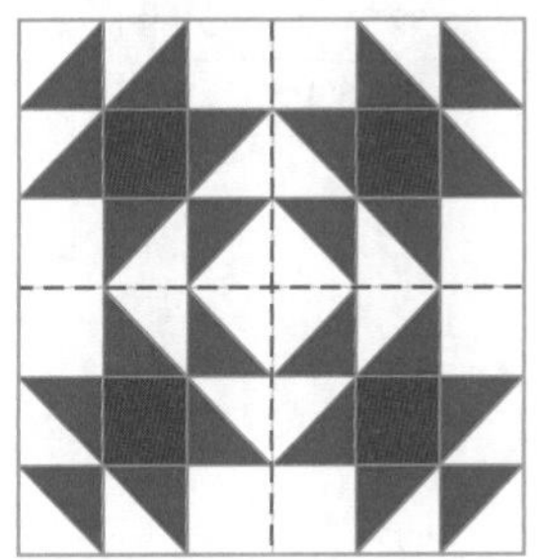

3 a 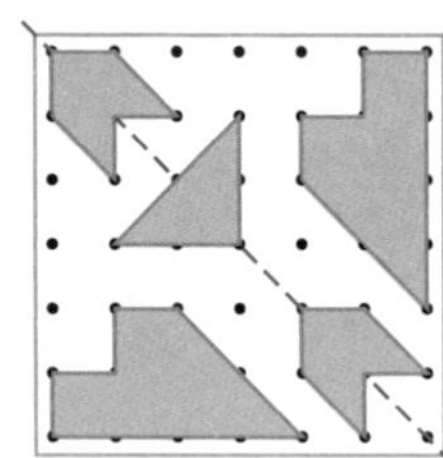 b 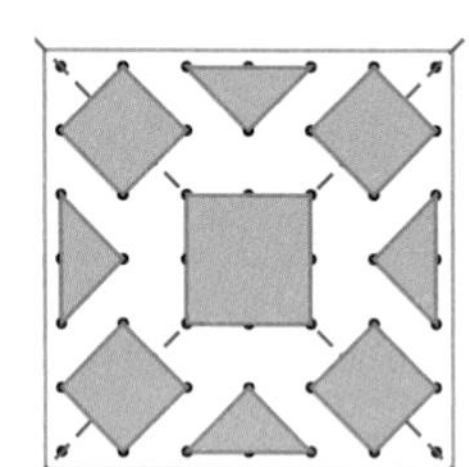

Go and do!

1 Open

2

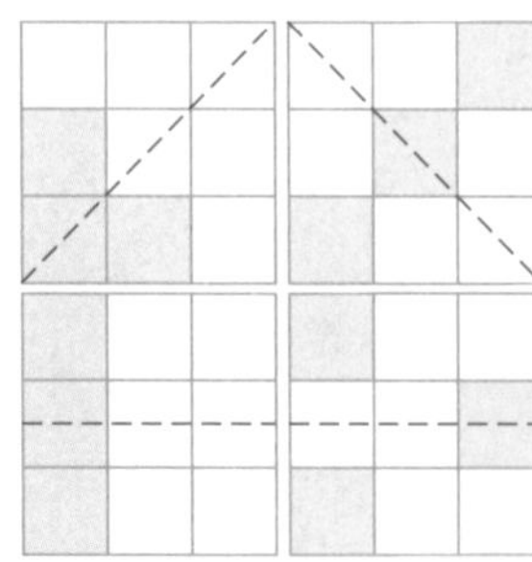
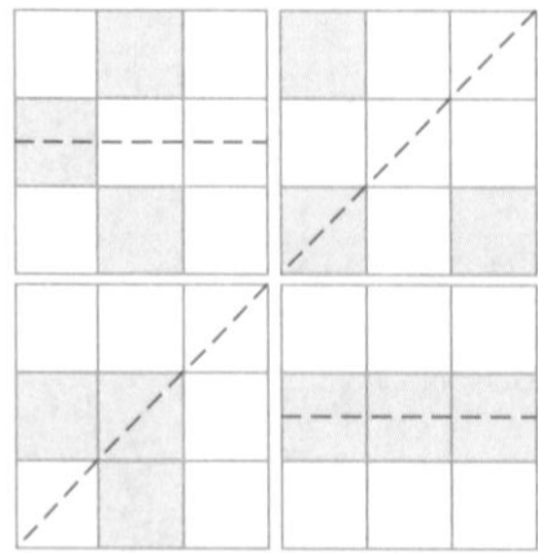
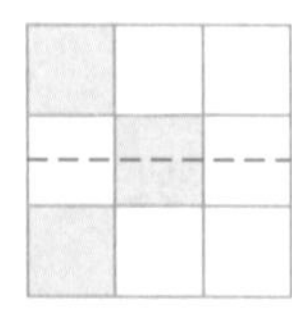
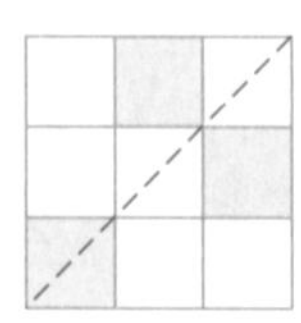

Pages 80–81 **Data collection**

Go and do!

1, 2 and 3 Open

Pages 82–83 **Pie charts**

1 a Post b Herald c Echo

2 a

When did you last visit your dental surgery?	Percentage of children	Number of children
a in the last 3 months	26%	52
b 3–6 months ago	44%	88
c more than 6 months ago	16%	32
d over 1 year ago	14%	28

b

What was the reason for your last visit?	Percentage of children	Number of children
a in pain	37%	74
b regular check-up with dentist	26%	52
c filling or extraction	15%	30
d straightening teeth	22%	44

c

How often do you brush your teeth?	Percentage of children	Number of children
a less than once a day	7%	14
b once a day	23%	46
c twice a day	54%	108
d more than twice a day	16%	32

Go and do! Open

Pages 84–85 **Conversion graphs**

1 a

Miles	0	5	10	15	20
Kilometres	0	8	16	24	32
Co-ordinates	(0, 0)	(5, 8)	(10, 16)	(15, 24)	(20, 32)

c 45 miles ≈ 72 km 64 km ≈ 40 miles
75 miles ≈ 120 km 30 km ≈ 18.75 miles

d 250 miles ≈ 400 km 350 miles ≈ 560 km 1010 miles ≈ 1616 km

e **Distances from Inverness**

Town	miles	km
Aberdeen	103	165
Ayr	200	320
Fort William	65	104
Glasgow	168	269
Ullapool	55	88
Thurso	110	176

Go and do!

1, 2 Open

Pages 86–87 **Probability**

1 a 3 red, 3 blue faces b 2 red, 2 blue and 2 green faces

c

Event	Chance	Probability
Red	1 in 6	$\frac{1}{6}$
Blue	2 in 6	$\frac{1}{3}$
Green	3 in 6	$\frac{1}{2}$

2 copper – unlikely silver – likely heptagonal – unlikely
less than £2 – certain more than 5p – even 2p coin – impossible

Go and do!

1 Possible solutions

Event	Chance	Probability
£1	1 in 12	$\frac{1}{12}$
50p	2 in 12	$\frac{1}{6}$
20p	2 in 12	$\frac{1}{6}$
10p	1 in 12	$\frac{1}{12}$
5p	3 in 12	$\frac{1}{4}$
1p	3 in 12	$\frac{1}{4}$

2 Open

Positive and negative numbers

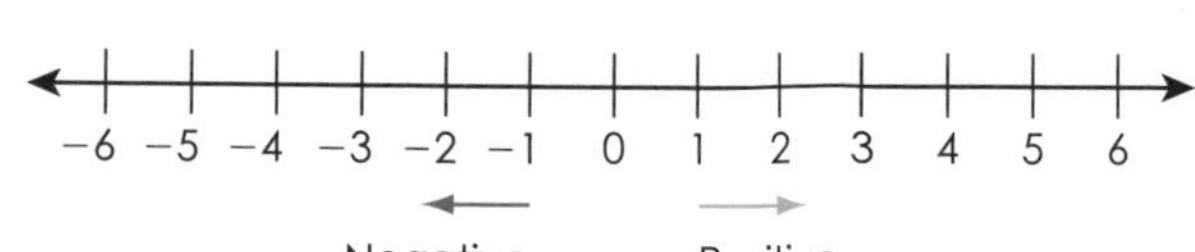

Fractions, decimals and percentages

$\frac{1}{10} = \frac{10}{100} = 0{\cdot}1 = 10\%$

$\frac{1}{5} = \frac{20}{100} = 0{\cdot}2 = 20\%$

$\frac{1}{20} = \frac{5}{100} = 0{\cdot}05 = 5\%$

$\frac{1}{2} = \frac{50}{100} = 0{\cdot}5 = 50\%$

$\frac{1}{4} = \frac{25}{100} = 0{\cdot}25 = 25\%$

$\frac{3}{4} = \frac{75}{100} = 0{\cdot}75 = 75\%$

$\frac{1}{8} = \frac{125}{1000} = 0{\cdot}125 = 12\frac{1}{2}\%$

$\frac{1}{3} \approx 0{\cdot}333 = 33\frac{1}{3}\%$

$\frac{2}{3} \approx 0{\cdot}667 = 66\frac{2}{3}\%$

Multiplication and division facts

	×1	×2	×3	×4	×5	×6	×7	×8	×9	×10
×1	1	2	3	4	5	6	7	8	9	10
×2	2	4	6	8	10	12	14	16	18	20
×3	3	6	9	12	15	18	21	24	27	30
×4	4	8	12	16	20	24	28	32	36	40
×5	5	10	15	20	25	30	35	40	45	50
×6	6	12	18	24	30	36	42	48	54	60
×7	7	14	21	28	35	42	49	56	63	70
×8	8	16	24	32	40	48	56	64	72	80
×9	9	18	27	36	45	54	63	72	81	90
×10	10	20	30	40	50	60	70	80	90	100

Tests of divisibility

2 Last digit is 0, 2, 4, 6 or 8.

3 Sum of the digits is divisible by 3.

4 Last two digits are divisible by 4.

5 Last digit is 5 or 0.

6 It is divisible by both 2 and 3.

8 Half of it is divisible by 4 *or* last 3 digits are divisible by 8.

9 Sum of the digits is divisible by 9.

10 Last digit is 0.

Length

1 km = 1000 m = 100 000 cm

0·1 km = 100 m = 10 000 cm

0·01 km = 10 m = 1000 cm

1 m = 100 cm = 1000 mm

0·1 m = 10 cm = 100 mm

0·01 m = 1 cm = 10 mm

1 cm = 10 mm

0·1 cm = 1 mm

Mass

1 kg = 1000 g

0·1 kg = 100 g

0·01 kg = 10 g

0·001 kg = 1 g

Capacity

1 ℓ = 1000 ml

0·1 ℓ = 100 ml

0·01 ℓ = 10 ml

0·001 ℓ = 1 ml

1 cℓ = 10 ml

Perimeter and area

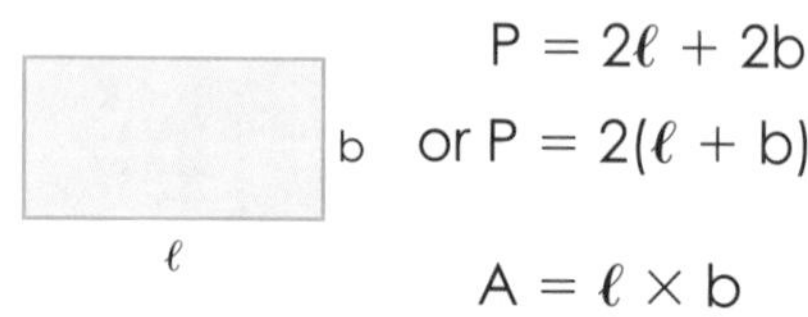

$P = 2\ell + 2b$

or $P = 2(\ell + b)$

$A = \ell \times b$

Volume

cuboid

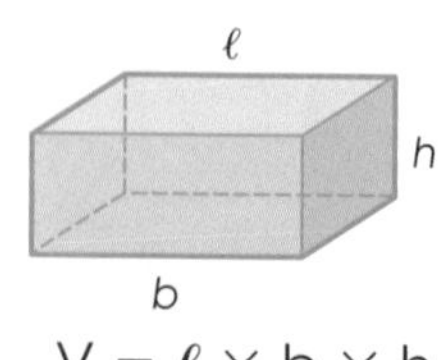

$V = \ell \times b \times h$

cube

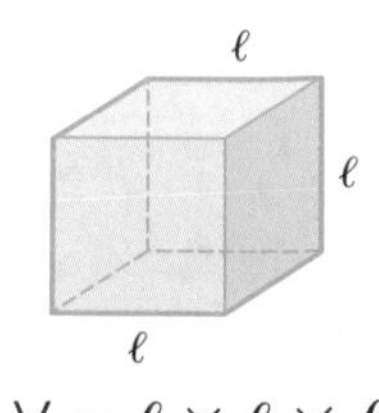

$V = \ell \times \ell \times \ell$

24 hour clock

Time, speed and distance

Distance $D = S \times T$

Speed $S = \frac{D}{T} = D \div T$

Time $T = \frac{D}{S} = D \div S$

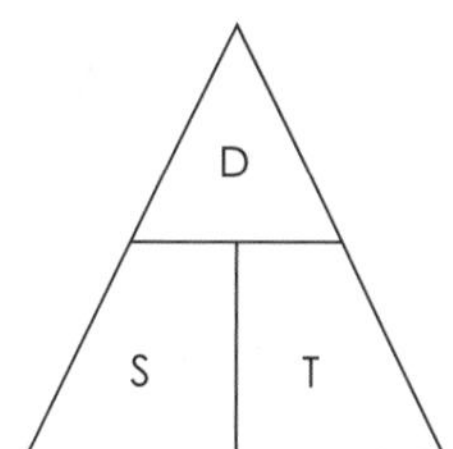

Addition

4826 + 6439

$$\begin{array}{r} 4826 \\ +\ 6439 \\ \hline 11265 \\ {\scriptstyle 1\ \ 1} \end{array}$$

26·48 + 5·375

$$\begin{array}{r} 26{\cdot}48 \\ +\ 5{\cdot}375 \\ \hline 31{\cdot}855 \\ {\scriptstyle 1\ \ 1} \end{array}$$

Subtraction

7845 − 2367

$$\begin{array}{r} {\scriptstyle 7\,13\,15} \\ 7845 \\ -\ 2367 \\ \hline 5478 \end{array}$$

67·58 − 43·69

$$\begin{array}{r} {\scriptstyle 6\ 14\,18} \\ 67{\cdot}58 \\ -\ 43{\cdot}69 \\ \hline 23{\cdot}89 \end{array}$$

Short multiplication

5697 × 8

$$\begin{array}{r} 5697 \\ \times\ 8 \\ \hline 45576 \end{array}$$

865·56 × 7

$$\begin{array}{r} 865{\cdot}56 \\ \times\ 7 \\ \hline 6058{\cdot}92 \end{array}$$

Short division

337 ÷ 8

$$8\,\overline{)\,33^{1}7}\quad = 42\text{ R}1$$

48·6 ÷ 3

$$3\,\overline{)\,48{\cdot}6}\quad = 16{\cdot}2$$

Order of operations

Brackets → Multiplication → Division → Addition → Subtraction

e.g. 10 − (3 + 4) = 3 (10 − 3) + 4 = 11 10 × (3 + 4) = 70 (10 × 3) + 4 = 34

Factors

The factors of 12 are 1, 2, 3, 4, 6 and 12 as they all divide exactly into 12. Factors of 12 can be put into pairs.
1 × 12 = 12, 2 × 6 = 12, 3 × 4 = 12

Multiples

10, 20, 30, 40, 15 are all multiples of 10 as we can divide 10 into them all. They are also multiples of 2 and 5. Each number is exactly divisible by 2 or 5.

2D shapes

circle

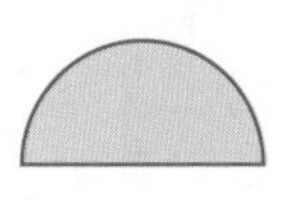
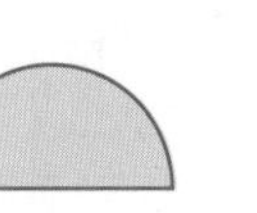
semi-circle

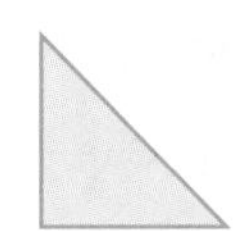
right-angled triangle

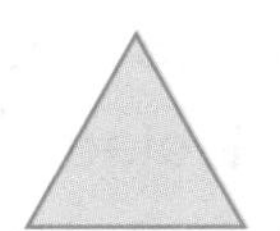
equilateral triangle

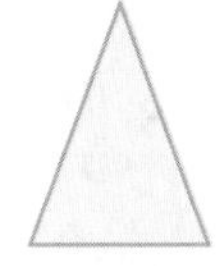
isosceles triangle

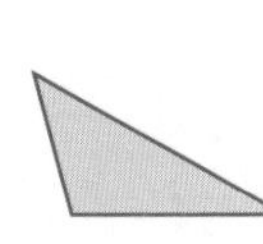
scalene triangle

square

rectangle

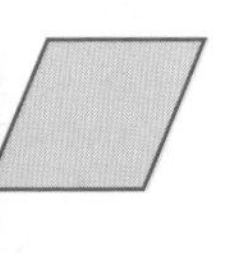
rhombus

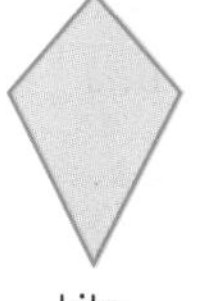
kite

parallelogram

trapezium

pentagon

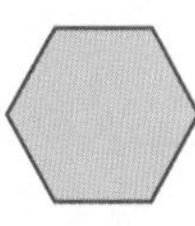
hexagon

heptagon

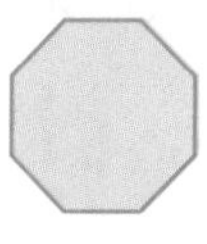
octagon

3D solids

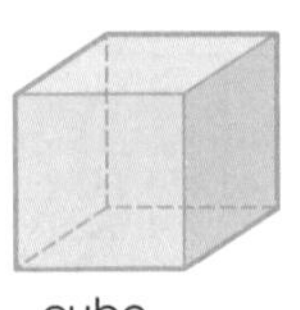
cube

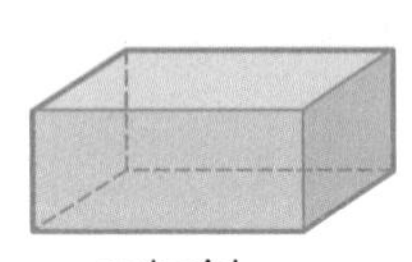
cuboid

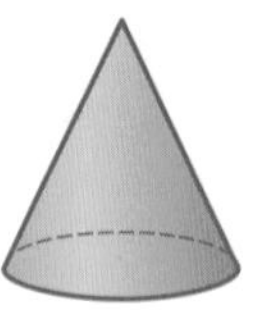
cone

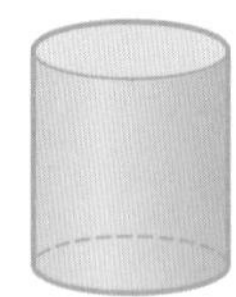
cylinder

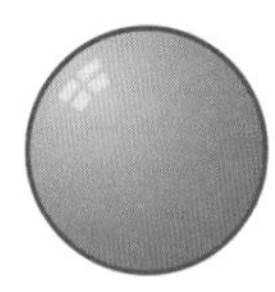
sphere

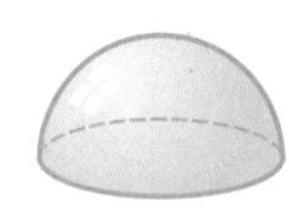
hemi-sphere

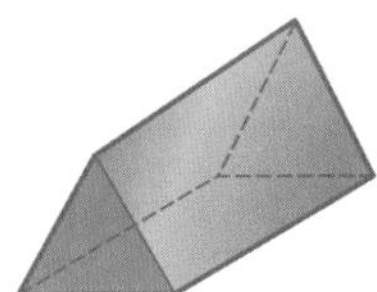
triangular prism

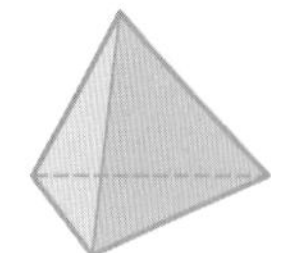
triangular-based pyramid (tetrahedron)

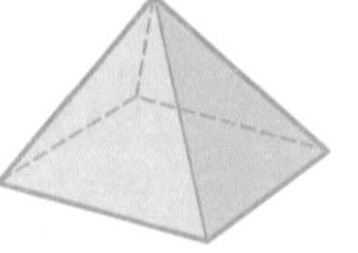
square-based pyramid

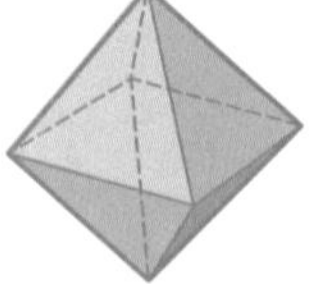
octahedron

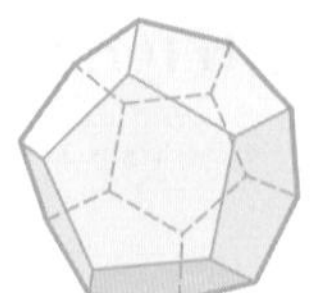
dodecahedron

Angles

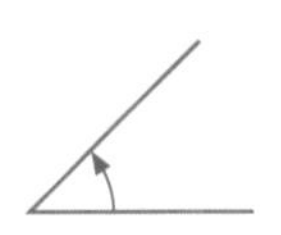
An acute angle is between 0° and 90°.

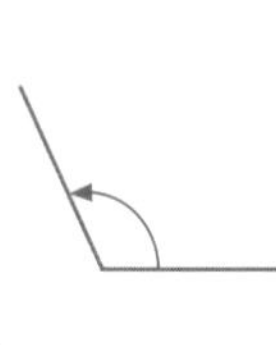
An obtuse angle is between 90° and 180°.

A reflex angle is between 180° and 270°.

A right angle is is 90°.

Angles on a straight line add up to 180°.

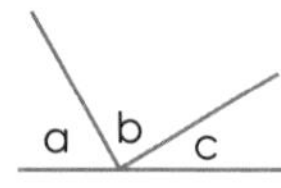

Angles in a triangle add up to 180°.

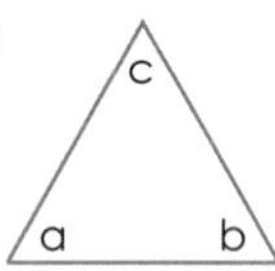

Angles at a point add up to 360°.

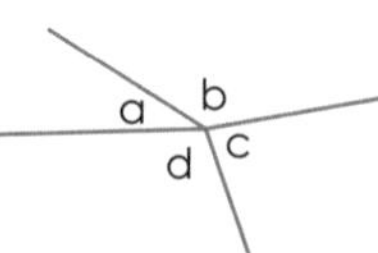

Lines

Parallel lines

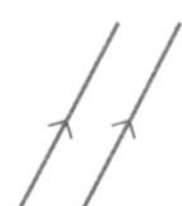

Perpendicular lines

Compass rose

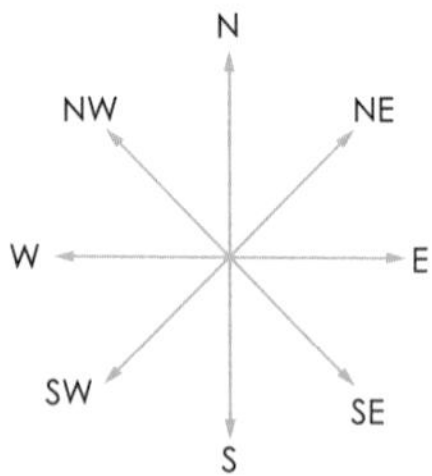

Co-ordinates

Along 5
up 3
A (5, 3)

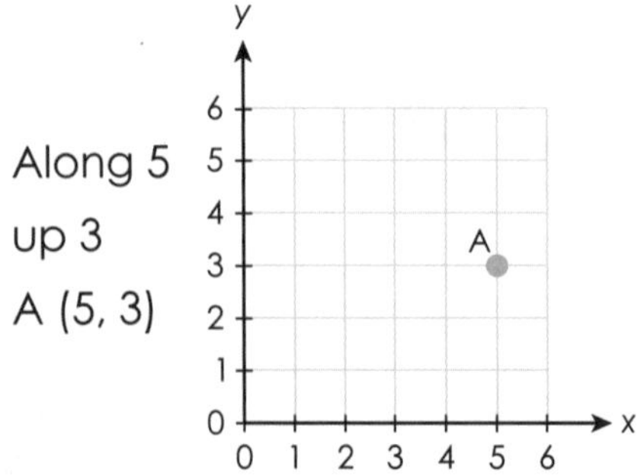

Reflection

Shape A has been reflected along the diagonal line of symmetry

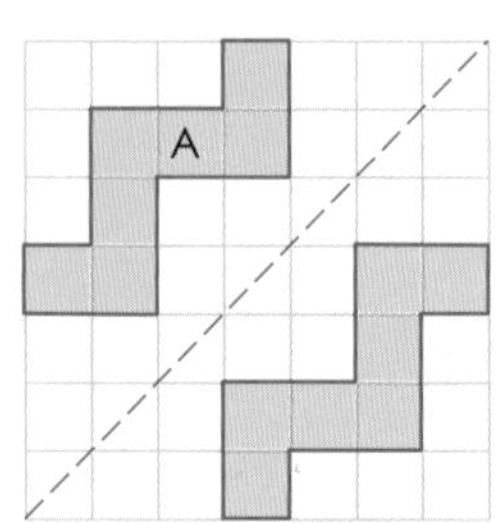